175 fruit desserts

175 fruit desserts

Delicious easy-to-follow recipes, with more than 200 glorious colour photographs showing everything from elegant sorbets to comforting hot crumbles and pies

Edited by Ann Kay

southwater

This edition is published by Southwater

Southwater is an imprint of Anness Publishing Ltd
Hermes House, 88–89 Blackfriars Road, London SE1 8HA
tel. 020 7401 2077; fax 020 7633 9499
www.southwaterbooks.com; www.annesspublishing.com

If you like the images in this book and would like to investigate using them
for publishing, promotions or advertising, please visit our website
www.practicalpictures.com for more information.

© Anness Publishing Ltd 2006

UK agent: The Manning Partnership Ltd, 6 The Old Dairy, Melcombe Road,
Bath BA2 3LR; tel. 01225 478444; fax 01225 478440;
sales@manning-partnership.co.uk

UK distributor: Grantham Book Services Ltd, Isaac Newton Way,
Alma Park Industrial Estate, Grantham, Lincs NG31 9SD;
tel. 01476 541080; fax 01476 541061; orders@gbs.tbs-ltd.co.uk

North American agent/distributor: National Book Network,
4501 Forbes Boulevard, Suite 200, Lanham, MD 20706;
tel. 301 459 3366; fax 301 429 5746; www.nbnbooks.com

Australian agent/distributor: Pan Macmillan Australia, Level 18,
St Martins Tower, 31 Market St, Sydney, NSW 2000;
tel. 1300 135 113; fax 1300 135 103; customer.service@macmillan.com.au

New Zealand agent/distributor: David Bateman Ltd, 30 Tarndale Grove,
Off Bush Road, Albany, Auckland; tel. (09) 415 7664; fax (09) 415 8892

Publisher: Joanna Lorenz
Editorial Director: Helen Sudell
Editors: Ann Kay and Elizabeth Woodland
Copy-editor: Julia Canning
Design: Diane Pullen and Design Principals
Production Controller: Lee Sargeant

1 3 5 7 9 10 8 6 4 2

NOTES

Bracketed terms are intended for American readers.

For all recipes, quantities are given in both metric and imperial measures and,
where appropriate, in standard cups and spoons. Follow one set, but not a
mixture, because they are not interchangeable.

Standard spoon and cup measures are level. 1 tsp = 5ml,
1 tbsp = 15ml, 1 cup = 250ml/8fl oz.

Australian standard tablespoons are 20ml. Australian readers
should use 3 tsp in place of 1 tbsp for measuring small quantities
of gelatine, flour, salt, etc.

American pints are 16fl oz/2 cups. American readers should use
20fl oz/2.5 cups in place of 1 pint when measuring liquids.

Electric oven temperatures in this book are for conventional ovens.
When using a fan oven, the temperature will probably need to be reduced
by about 10–20°C/20–40°F. Since ovens vary, you should check with your
manufacturer's instruction book for guidance.

The nutritional analysis given for each recipe is calculated per portion (i.e.
serving or item), unless otherwise stated. If the recipe gives a range, such as
Serves 4–6, then the nutritional analysis will be for the smaller portion size,
i.e. 6 servings. Measurements for sodium do not include salt added to taste.

Medium (US large) eggs are used unless otherwise stated.

**Important: pregnant women, the elderly, the ill and very young
children should avoid recipes using raw or lightly cooked eggs.**

Main front cover image shows Frozen Clementines –
for recipe, see page 34.

Contents

Introduction   6

Working with Pastry   8

Preparing Fruit   10

Dessert Sauces   12

Hot Treats   14

Cool and Refreshing   34

Healthy Options   56

Quick and Easy   80

Index   96

Introduction

Fruit desserts are always popular, whether they are sumptuous creations or the simplest of dishes. Indeed, a well-chosen dessert is guaranteed to round off a meal on a high note and can

turn even the most ordinary meal into a memorable occasion. As a finale, a mouthwatering fruit tart, a delicately flavoured sorbet or ice cream or a rich and luxurious chocolate treat will delight guests and give you, the cook, great satisfaction.

Whether you are planning an elaborate dinner party or an everyday family meal, the key to success is to make sure that the dessert you select balances perfectly with the main course. If you are serving a filling or rich main course you will need to choose a delicate or fruity option to follow, while you can afford to indulge in a rich, creamy dessert if you opt for a light main dish. With the fantastic selection of recipes featured in this book, you will never be at a loss for ideas to create a perfectly balanced menu.

The other factors that might affect your choice of dessert, such as health concerns and the amount of time you have for preparation, are also catered for in this collection. Many of the desserts can be made a day or two in advance, others can be started early in the day and finished off just before you eat, while frozen desserts and ice creams can be made weeks in advance, ready to serve whenever you need them. When entertaining, the more preparation you can do ahead, the better, as this means that you will have time to enjoy the meal as much as your guests. However, there's also a wide choice of quick-to-make recipes that can be rustled up in a matter of minutes – so when time is short, or guests arrive unexpectedly, you need never miss out on the pleasure of a delicious dessert.

As a back-up to the recipes in this book, the introductory pages provide helpful information on preparing and baking pastry for pies and tarts, plus an invaluable guide to preparing fruit, from making perfect orange segments to creating delicate decorations. There are also ideas for easy dessert sauces to help you whip up instant desserts, plus clever finishing touches that will help you to achieve professional presentation. All the recipes in this book have clear, step-by-step instructions, so that even dishes that are commonly regarded as tricky, such as soufflés and strudels,

are easy to make and will look and taste delicious. The important thing is to read the whole recipe through before you start, so that you understand all the steps involved and can plan the preparation properly. A large number of recipes have helpful Cook's Tips and Variations, offering advice on specific aspects of a dish or interesting alternatives to get your imagination going or to help out when you don't necessarily have all the specified ingredients to hand.

The recipe chapters feature over 175 tempting fruit dishes, grouped in categories including Hot Treats, and Cool and Refreshing, as well as desserts reflecting our modern lives, such as Healthy Options and Quick and Easy chapters. Popular classics feature alongside more unusual recipes that are destined to become new favourites. Most of the recipes have a full-colour photograph, showing clearly the kind of end result that you are aiming to achieve.

Have fun leafing through these pages at any time of year and for any occasion. For summer days you can't go wrong with a cooling Watermelon Sorbet or a Scented Red & Orange Fruit Salad, while Toffee Bananas, Lemon Surprise Pudding and Strawberry & Apple Crumble are warming choices for winter. Instant entertaining is provided by Frudités with Honey Dip, or Chargrilled Apples on Cinnamon Toasts. International classics range from Brazilian Coffee Bananas to Thai-Fried Pineapple. Whether you are a novice or an experienced chef, are in a hurry, on a budget, preparing a mid-week family meal or catering for a lavish or important event, this collection of fruity desserts will provide all the answers, and indulge every taste.

Working with Pastry

Making your own pastry may seem daunting at first, but if you follow a few basic rules and stick to the right quantities, you will soon find the technique easy. The key is not to hurry and to keep your hands cool when handling the dough. The crisp, light results are always worth the effort and the popularity of your home-made tarts and pies will be truly satisfying.

SHORTCRUST PASTRY

With shortcrust pastry and its variations, once the dough has been formed into a ball, it is usually chilled for about 20 minutes to make handling easier. After the pastry has been rolled out and used to line a tin (pan), it should be chilled again to minimize shrinkage during baking. A filled tart or pie needs only about 30 minutes otherwise the pastry will turn soggy. An empty shell, prior to blind baking, can be chilled for longer.

Heating the Oven

Whatever type of pastry you are baking, always allow time to preheat the oven; it will take about 15 minutes to reach the required temperature (fan ovens may heat more quickly). If you are baking blind or cooking a double-crust pie, it's a good idea to put a heavy baking sheet in the oven to heat up. The hot baking sheet will give the base of the pie an initial blast of heat to help keep the base crisp. It will also make it easier to slide the dish in and out of the oven.

Baking Shortcrust Pastry

Shortcrust pastries are usually baked at 200°C/400°F/Gas 6, but the temperature is often reduced part-way through baking to allow the filling to cook sufficiently. As a general rule, bake pastry in the middle of the oven, or just above the middle, unless the recipe tells you otherwise. Take care with pastries that contain added sugar; they should be removed from the oven as soon as they are golden, because they can burn quickly at this stage.

Baking Rules

When following a recipe, baking times may vary slightly depending on your oven and how chilled the pie was before cooking. Always check the pie at least 5 minutes before the end of the suggested cooking time. Don't keep opening the oven door though, or the temperature will drop and the pastry will not be as crisp. Avoid cooking the pastry with other foods that release a lot of steam as this also prevents a crisp result.

Baking Blind

This process is used for a number of reasons. It is used to partly cook an empty pastry case so that it does not become soggy when the filling is added and the final baking is done. It is also used to completely bake a pastry case when the filling cooks in a relatively short time and you need to ensure that the pastry is fully cooked through. The process is also required when the pastry case is to contain a precooked mixture or an uncooked filling. Lining the pastry case with baking parchment or foil and filling it with baking beans stops the pastry from rising up during cooking.

1 Cut out a round of baking parchment or foil about 7.5cm/3in larger than the flan tin (tart pan). Prick the base of the pastry all over with a fork.

2 Lay the baking parchment or foil in the pastry case and press it smoothly over the base and up the side.

3 Put either the commercially made ceramic baking beans, or dried beans or peas, in the case, spreading them out evenly to cover the base. Whichever kind you choose, they can be used over and over again.

4 To partially bake the pastry, bake in an oven preheated to 200°C/400°F/Gas 6 for 15 minutes, or until the pastry is set and the rim is dry and golden. Remove and lift out the paper and beans. Return the case to the oven for a further 5 minutes. The pastry case can now be filled and the baking completed.

5 For fully baked pastry, bake the case at 200°C/400°F/Gas 6 for 15 minutes, then remove the paper and beans and return to the oven. Bake for a further 5–10 minutes, or until golden brown. Cool completely before filling.

6 To bake tartlets, bake blind in the same way as flans, but allow only 6–8 minutes for partial baking, and 12–15 minutes for fully baked pastry.

Cook's Tip

Fully baked pastry cases, both large and small, may be baked up to two days ahead if carefully stored in airtight containers. Interleave them with greaseproof (waxed) paper, or use baking parchment, if you are keeping several, and always make sure that they are cooled before storing.

Cook's Tips

• When moving rolled-out pastry dough to line a tin (pan) or dish or top a pie, roll the dough loosely around the rolling pin, lift up, then carefully unroll it on top of the container. Press gently in place.

• If you find any small holes in a cooked pastry case, repair them by brushing with a little beaten egg, then return the case to the oven for 2–3 minutes to seal. Any larger holes or tears that appear during baking should be repaired by pressing a little raw pastry in the gap, brushing with beaten egg, and then returning to the oven.

• If the pastry starts to bubble up during baking, remove from the oven, prick again with a fork to allow the trapped air to escape and return to the oven. If it has bubbled up when you take it out after cooking, don't try to press it flat, or you will crack the pastry. Make a very small slit in the case with a knife and leave it to shrink back on its own.

• If the pastry becomes fully browned before the filling has cooked through completely, then you should protect it by covering with foil. Cover single- or double-crust pies completely, but make a hole in the top of the foil to allow the steam to escape. When baking open flans, cover the pastry edge only – by using strips of foil.

PUFF PASTRY

The baking method for puff, rough puff and flaky pastry has much in common with that used for shortcrust. Chilling the pastry before baking is essential, and shaped puff pastries should be chilled for at least an hour to prevent the pastry becoming mis-shapen during baking. Take great care when brushing the pastry with egg glaze; any that runs down the sides of the pastry will make the layers stick together and prevent the pastry from rising well and evenly.

Oven Temperature

This type of pastry must be cooked in a preheated hot oven, so that the air trapped within the layers expands and lifts up the pastry. If the oven is too cool, the butter will melt before the dough has a chance to cook, and the pastry will not rise well. The oven temperature is usually 230°C/450°F/Gas 8, but small pastries are sometimes cooked at 220°C/425°F/Gas 7. Reduce the temperature after about 15 minutes, to give the filling time to cook through.

Releasing Steam

When baking puff pastry pies, up to three slits or holes (depending how moist the filling is) should be made in the pastry top to allow the steam from the filling to escape. Don't make too many steam holes though, or too much air will be lost and the pastry won't rise well. After baking, cover steam holes with cooked pastry decorations.

Unlike shortcrust pastries, a steamy atmosphere helps the puff pastry to rise. Put a dish of hot water on the lowest shelf when preheating the oven. Remove it for the last few minutes of cooking. If the pastry starts to sink after cooking, it hasn't cooked sufficiently and should be returned to the oven for a little longer.

FILO PASTRY

Unlike shortcrust and puff pastries, filo pastry does not require chilling before baking. The most important point to remember is that filo must never dry out, or it will become brittle and hard to fold and shape. Keep the sheets you are not working with covered with a damp dish towel. It may also crumble if it is too cold so, before using, remove the unopened packet from the refrigerator and allow to stand for 1 hour.

Filo must always be lightly brushed with melted butter before baking to give it a shiny glaze; unsalted (sweet) butter is ideal because it has a lower water content than ordinary butter, or oil can also be used. Choose a mild-flavoured oil when making sweet pastries as you do not want the flavour of the oil to overpower delicate tastes. Be careful not to overdo the melted fat; it should be brushed as thinly and evenly as possible to create light crisp layers. Never brush filo with egg or milk as this would make it soggy.

Oven Temperature

The usual temperature for baking filo pastry is 200°C/400°F/Gas 6, although it can be cooked at a slightly lower temperature without its crisp texture being affected. Filo pastry colours very quickly, so always check frequently towards the end of the cooking time. If the pastry has browned sufficiently before the filling is cooked, cover it loosely with foil, then remove again for the last few minutes to make sure the top of the pie is dry and crisp.

Leftover Filo Pastry

Wrap any unused filo in clear film (plastic wrap) and return it to the refrigerator. It will keep for seven to ten days. It is possible to re-freeze filo, but don't do this more than once.

Preparing Fruit

Fresh fruit provides the perfect base for all manner of delicious and healthy desserts. To make the most of the different types of fruit, there are certain preparation techniques that will always be useful, whether you are making a fresh fruit salad or creating a more elaborate dessert. For professional results, just follow the step instructions below.

BUYING FRUIT

Obviously, the best time to buy fruit is when it is fully ripe and at its peak. The exceptions are fruits such as bananas and pears, which ripen quickly and can therefore be bought in an under-ripe condition and allowed to ripen fully at home. You are most likely to find top-quality fruits in markets and stores that have a quick turnover of fresh produce, preferably with a daily delivery. Although most fruits are now available almost all the year round, they are nearly always best and cheapest when in season in the country of origin. Only buy as much fruit as you need at one time so that it remains fresh and appetizing.

PREPARING FRUIT

For some fruits, the only preparation needed is washing or wiping with a damp cloth; others must be peeled, cored, stoned (pitted) or seeded. Wash fruit only just before using. If necessary, cut away any bruised or damaged parts.

Peeling Firm Fruit

Some firm fruits, such as eating apples and pears, can be served raw without peeling. For cooking, peeling is often necessary. Pare off the skin as thinly as possible to avoid losing the valuable nutrients under the skin.

1 To peel fruit, first wash it and then pat it dry by using kitchen paper. Use a small, sharp paring knife or a vegetable peeler to pare off the skin in long, thin vertical strips all round the fruit, making sure that you cut into the fruit as thinly as possible. Pears in particular are best peeled by this method.

2 Alternatively, for apples, thinly peel all round the fruit in a spiral.

Coring Firm Fruit

1 To core whole apples and pears, place the sharp edge of a corer over the stem end of the fruit.

2 Press the corer down firmly into the fruit, and then twist it slightly; the core, complete with all of the pips (seeds), should come away in the centre of the corer. Now push out the corer from the handle end to remove the complete core cleanly.

Segmenting Firm Fruit

1 Halve the fruit lengthways, then cut into quarters or segments.

2 Now cut out the central core and pips using a small, sharp knife, taking care not to cut yourself as you work the knife towards you.

Cook's Tip

Some fruits, such as apples, pears and bananas, quickly oxidize and turn brown when exposed to the air. To prevent discoloration, brush cut fruits with lemon juice. Alternatively, acidulate a bowl of cold water by stirring in the juice of half a lemon. Drop the cut fruits into the bowl immediately after preparing.

Peeling Citrus Fruit

It is very important to remove all of the bitter white pith that lies just beneath the rind of citrus fruits.

1 To peel firm-skinned fruits, hold the fruit over a bowl to catch the juice and use a sharp knife to cut off the rind.

2 Alternatively, cut a slice off the top and bottom of the fruit, place on a board and, cutting downwards, slice off the rind in strips,

3 For loose-skinned fruit, such as tangerines, pierce the skin with your forefinger at the stalk end and peel off the rind. Pull off all the white shreds adhering to the fruit.

Segmenting Citrus Fruit

1 Using a small serrated knife, cut down between the membranes enclosing the segments; ease out the flesh.

Grating Citrus Fruit Rind

1 For finely grated rind, grate it against the fine face of a grater. Remove only the coloured rind; if you grate too deeply into the peel, you will be in danger of including the bitter white pith.

2 For thinly pared strips of rind, use a cannelle knife (zester) or vegetable peeler, then cut into shreds if necessary.

Decorating with Citrus Fruit

1 To make thick julienne strips of rind, cut lengthways, using a cannelle knife.

2 To make twists, slice the fruits thinly, cut to the centre, then twist the ends in opposite directions to make an S-shape.

Peeling Soft Fruit

Fruits such as peaches, nectarines and apricots can be peeled with a sharp paring knife, but this may waste some of the delicious flesh. It is better to loosen the skins by dipping them briefly in boiling water.

1 To remove the skins quickly and cleanly from peaches, nectarines and apricots, start by making a tiny nick in the skin, using the point of a sharp knife. This is done in order to help the skins spring off the flesh when the fruits are immersed in water. Take care when you are handling the soft fruit as the flesh can be easily damaged by clutching the fruit too firmly.

2 Cover with boiling water and leave for 15–30 seconds, depending on the ripeness of the fruit. Remove the fruit with a slotted spoon and peel off the skin, which should come away easily.

Removing Stones (Pits) and Seeds

1 Cut all round the fruit through the seam. Twist the halves in opposite directions, then lever out the stone (pit).

2 To pit cherries, simply place a cherry in a cherry stoner and then push the bar firmly into the fruit. The pit will be neatly ejected.

3 To remove the seeds from grapes, first cut the grapes in half, and then pick out the tiny pips using the tip of a small sharp knife.

4 To remove either papaya or melon seeds, you should first cut the fruit in half using a sharp knife, and then neatly scoop out all of the seeds with a spoon.

Dessert Sauces

Fresh custards and flavoured sweet white sauces are classic dessert sauces, but quick and easy dessert toppings can be made almost instantly from ready-made ingredients. These are ideal to serve over scoops of ice cream or with crêpes to create no-fuss desserts. Simple sauces can also be used imaginatively to create special finishing touches for desserts.

USING VANILLA PODS (BEANS)
Vanilla pods are often used in sweet dessert sauces – most commonly to flavour milk, cream or sugar.

Vanilla Infusions
1 To flavour milk or cream with vanilla for a sauce, put the milk or cream in a pan, add the whole vanilla pod and heat gently over a low heat until almost boiling. Remove from the heat, cover and leave to stand for 10 minutes. Remove the pod, rinse and dry; it may be re-used several times.

2 To get maximum flavour, use a sharp knife to slit the pod lengthways, then open it out. Use the tip of the knife to scrape out the sticky black seeds inside: add to the hot sauce.

Vanilla Sugar
Many dessert sauces benefit from the delicate flavour of vanilla-flavoured sugar. This is available ready-made from shops but it is easy to make your own version.

1 To make vanilla sugar, simply bury a vanilla pod in a jar of white sugar. Cover tightly for a few weeks until the sugar takes on the vanilla flavour. Shake the jar occasionally.

SPEEDY SAUCES FOR TOPPING ICE CREAM
Store-cupboard (pantry) ingredients can often be transformed into irresistible sauces to spoon on top of ice cream.

Marshmallow Melt

1 Melt 90g/3½oz marshmallows with 30ml/2 tbsp milk or cream in a small pan. Add a little grated nutmeg and stir until smooth. Serve immediately.

Black Forest Sauce

1 Drain a can of black cherries, reserving the juice. Blend a little of the juice with a little arrowroot or cornflour (cornstarch).

2 Add the cornflour mixture to the rest of the juice in a pan. Stir until boiling and lightly thickened, then add the cherries and a dash of Kirsch and heat through.

Raspberry Coulis
1 Purée some thawed frozen raspberries, with icing (confectioners') sugar to taste, then press through a sieve (strainer).

2 Blend a little cornflour (cornstarch) with some orange juice, and stir into the purée; cook for 2 minutes until thick. Cool.

Chocolate-Toffee Sauce

1 Chop a Mars bar and heat very gently in a pan, stirring until just melted. Spoon over scoops of vanilla ice cream and sprinkle with chopped nuts.

Marmalade Whisky Sauce

1 Heat 60ml/4 tbsp chunky marmalade in a pan with 30ml/2 tbsp whisky, until just melted. Allow to bubble for a few seconds then spoon over ice cream.

Nutty Butterscotch Sauce
1 Melt 75g/3oz/6 tbsp butter and 175g/6oz/¾ cup soft dark brown sugar in a heavy pan, then bring to the boil and boil for 2 minutes. Cool the mixture for 5 minutes.

2 Heat 175ml/6fl oz/¾ cup evaporated (unsweetened condensed) milk to just below boiling point, then gradually stir into the sugar mixture. Cook over a low heat for 2 minutes, stirring frequently.

3 Spread 50g/2oz/½ cup hazelnuts on a baking sheet and toast under a hot grill (broiler). Turn them on to a clean dish towel and rub off the skins. Chop the nuts roughly and stir into the sauce.

PRESENTATION IDEAS

When you've made a delicious sauce for a special dessert, why not make more of it by using it for decoration on the plate, too? Try one of the following simple ideas to make your sauce into a talking point. Individual slices of desserts, cakes or tarts, or a stuffed baked peach, look especially good served with sauce presented in this way.

Marbling

Use this technique when you have two contrasting sauces of a similar thickness, such as a fruit purée with cream or thin fresh custard.

I Spoon alternate spoonfuls of the two sauces on to a serving plate or shallow dish. Using a spoon, stir the sauces lightly together, gently swirling to create a marbled effect.

Yin-Yang Sauces

This oriental pattern is ideal for two contrasting colours of purée or coulis, such as a raspberry and a mango fruit coulis. It is important to make sure that the flavours of the sauce complement one another.

I Spoon a sauce on one side of a serving plate or shallow bowl. Add the second sauce to the other side, then gently push the two sauces together with the spoon, swirling one around the other, to make a yin-yang shape.

Drizzling

I Pour a smooth sauce or coulis into a container or tube with a fine pouring lip.

2 Drizzle the sauce in droplets or fine wavy lines on to the plate around the area where the dessert will sit.

Piping Outlines

I Spoon a small amount of fruit coulis or chocolate sauce into a piping (pastry) bag fitted with a plain writing nozzle.

2 Carefull

shape on to a serving plate, then spoon in the same sauce to fill the space within the outline.

Feathering Hearts

I Flood the plate with a smooth sauce such as chocolate sauce or fruit purée. Add small droplets of pouring cream into it at intervals.

2 Draw the tip of a small knife through the droplets of cream, to drag each drop into a heart.

QUICK SAUCES FOR CRÊPES

Give crêpes and pancakes a lift with these three easy ideas.

Rich Butterscotch Sauce

I Heat 75g/3oz/6 tbsp butter, 175g/6oz/¾ cup soft light brown sugar and 30ml/2 tbsp golden (light corn) syrup in a pan over a low heat until melted.

2 Remove from the heat and add 75ml/5 tbsp double (heavy) cream, stirring constantly, until smooth.

Orange Caramel Sauce

I Melt 25g/1oz/2 tbsp unsalted (sweet) butter in a heavy pan. Stir in 50g/2oz/¼ cup caster (superfine) sugar and cook until golden brown.

2 Add the juice of 2 oranges and ½ lemon; stir until the caramel has dissolved.

Summer Berry Sauce

I Melt 25g/1oz/2 tbsp butter in a frying pan. Add 50g/2oz/¼ cup caster (superfine) sugar and cook until golden.

2 Add the juice of 2 oranges and the rind of ½ orange and cook until syrupy. Add 350g/12oz/3 cups mixed summer berries and warm through.

3 Add 45ml/3 tbsp orange-flavoured liqueur and set alight. Serve immediately.

Chocolate Chip Banana Pancakes

These tasty little morsels will go down well with both adults and children alike.

Makes 16

2 ripe bananas
2 eggs
200ml/7fl oz/scant 1 cup milk
150g/5oz/1¼ cups self-raising (self-rising) flour, sifted
25g/1oz/⅓ cup ground almonds
15g/½oz/1 tbsp caster (superfine) sugar
pinch of salt
15ml/1 tbsp plain (semisweet) chocolate chips
butter, for frying
50g/2oz/½ cup toasted flaked (sliced) almonds

For the topping

150ml/¼ pint/⅔ cup double (heavy) cream
15g/½oz/1 tbsp icing (confectioners') sugar

1 Mash the bananas in a bowl. Beat in the eggs and half the milk. Mix in the flour, ground almonds, sugar and salt. Add the remaining milk and the chocolate chips.

2 Stir the mixture well until it makes a thick batter. Heat a knob (pat) of butter in a non-stick frying pan. Spoon the pancake mixture into the pan in heaps, allowing room for them to spread. When the pancakes are lightly browned underneath and bubbling on top, flip them over to cook the other side. Slide on to a plate and keep hot. Make more pancakes in the same way.

3 Make the topping. Pour the cream into a bowl. Add the icing sugar to sweeten it slightly, and whip to soft peaks. Spoon the cream on to the pancakes and decorate with flaked almonds. Serve immediately.

> **Cook's Tips**
> • *To toast flaked (sliced) almonds, simply put under the grill (broiler) for a few minutes, shaking the pan, until lightly golden.*
> • *You could add sliced banana, tossed in lemon juice, to the topping to enhance the banana flavour of the pancakes. If you prefer, use yogurt as a low-fat alternative to cream.*

Chocolate Amaretti Peaches

A delicious dish of peaches stuffed with chocolate. This is a simple dessert but nonetheless one that is simply bursting with Italian style and flavour.

Serves 4

115g/4oz amaretti, crushed
50g/2oz plain (semisweet) chocolate, chopped
finely grated rind of ½ orange
15ml/1 tbsp clear honey
1.5ml/¼ tsp ground cinnamon
1 egg white, lightly beaten
4 firm ripe peaches
150ml/¼ pint/⅔ cup white wine
15g/½oz/1 tbsp caster (superfine) sugar
whipped cream, to serve

1 Preheat the oven to 190°C/375°F/Gas 5. Mix together the crushed amaretti, chopped chocolate, orange rind, honey and cinnamon in a bowl. Add the beaten egg white and mix to bind the mixture.

2 Halve the peaches, remove the stones (pits) and fill the cavities with the chocolate mixture, mounding it up slightly.

3 Arrange the stuffed peaches in a lightly buttered, shallow ovenproof dish that will just hold the peaches comfortably.

4 Mix the wine and sugar in a jug (pitcher). Pour the wine mixture around the peaches.

5 Bake the peaches for 30–40 minutes, or until the peaches are tender when tested with a metal skewer and the filling has turned a golden colour.

6 Serve immediately with a little cooking juice spooned over. Accompany with cream.

> **Cook's Tip**
> • *To stone (pit) peaches, halve them and twist the two halves apart, then lever out the stone (pit) with the point of a knife.*

Choc. Pancakes Energy 192Kcal/798kJ; Protein 3.4g; Carbohydrate 13.7g, of which sugars 6.3g; Fat 14.1g, of which saturates 7.1g; Cholesterol 51mg; Calcium 70mg; Fibre 0.8g; Sodium 89mg.
Choc. Amar. Peaches Energy 282Kcal/1190kJ; Protein 4.1g; Carbohydrate 47g, of which sugars 34.4g; Fat 7.4g, of which saturates 3.8g; Cholesterol 1mg; Calcium 56mg; Fibre 2.4g; Sodium 117mg.

Baked Apples with Apricot Filling

Baked apples of all kinds have long been a top favourite. Here, this popular classic has been given a new twist with a refreshing apricot-flavoured filling.

Serves 6

75g/3oz/scant ½ cup chopped, ready-to-eat dried apricots

50g/2oz/½ cup chopped walnuts
5ml/1 tsp finely grated lemon rind
2.5ml/½ tsp ground cinnamon
90g/3½oz/½ cup soft light brown sugar
25g/1oz/2 tbsp butter, at room temperature
6 large eating apples
15ml/1 tbsp melted butter
natural (plain) yogurt, to serve

1 Preheat the oven to 190°C/375°F/Gas 5. Place the apricots, walnuts, lemon rind and cinnamon in a bowl. Add the sugar and butter and stir until thoroughly mixed.

2 Core the apples, without cutting all the way through to the base. Peel the top of each apple and then slightly widen the top of each opening to make room for the filling.

3 Spoon the filling into the apples, packing it down lightly.

4 Place the stuffed apples in an ovenproof dish large enough to hold them all comfortably side by side.

5 Brush the apples with the melted butter, then bake for 45–50 minutes, until they are tender. Serve hot, topped with spoonfuls of yogurt.

Cook's Tips
• *You can also use traditionally dried apricots for the filling, but they should be rehydrated first. Leave them to soak in warm water for 30 minutes or, for extra flavour, in dry white wine for 2 hours. Drain, squeeze out gently and chop.*
• *The easiest way to chop nuts is in a food processor or blender. Add 5ml/1 tsp of the sugar to stop them from sticking.*

Baked Apples with Caramel Sauce

A creamy caramel sauce transforms an old favourite.

Serves 6

3 green eating apples, cored but not peeled
3 red eating apples, cored but not peeled
175ml/6fl oz/¾ cup water
150g/5oz/¾ cup light brown sugar
2.5ml/½ tsp grated nutmeg

1.5ml/¼ tsp ground black pepper
40g/1½oz/¼ cup walnut pieces
40g/1½oz/scant ¼ cup sultanas (golden raisins)
50g/2oz/¼ cup butter, diced, plus extra for greasing

For the caramel sauce
15g/½oz/1 tbsp butter
120ml/4fl oz/½ cup whipping cream

1 Preheat the oven to 190°C/375°F/Gas 5. Grease an ovenproof dish just large enough to hold the apples.

2 With a small knife, cut at an angle to enlarge the core opening at the stem-end of each apple to about 2.5cm/1in in diameter. (The opening should resemble a funnel in shape.) Arrange the apples in the prepared dish, stem-end up.

3 In a small pan, combine the water with the brown sugar, nutmeg and pepper. Bring the mixture to the boil, stirring. Boil for 6 minutes.

4 Mix together the walnuts and sultanas. Spoon some of the walnut-sultana mixture into the opening in each apple. Top each apple with some of the diced butter or margarine.

5 Spoon the brown sugar sauce over and around the apples. Bake for 45–50 minutes, basting occasionally with the sauce, until the apples are just tender. Transfer the apples to a serving dish, reserving the sauce in the dish. Keep the apples warm.

6 For the caramel sauce, mix the butter, cream and reserved brown sugar sauce in a pan. Bring to the boil, stirring occasionally, and simmer for about 2 minutes until thickened. Leave the sauce to cool slightly before serving.

Baked Apples/Apricot Energy 239Kcal/1008kJ; Protein 2.3g; Carbohydrate 34.2g, of which sugars 34.1g; Fat 11.4g, of which saturates 3.9g; Cholesterol 14mg; Calcium 32mg; Fibre 3.5g; Sodium 47mg.
Baked Apples/Caramel Energy 430Kcal/1778kJ; Protein 2g; Carbohydrate 11.5g, of which sugars 11.5g; Fat 42.2g, of which saturates 24.1g; Cholesterol 97mg; Calcium 31mg; Fibre 1.4g; Sodium 225mg.

Peachy Chocolate Bake

A sublime combination of peaches and chocolate, this lightweight baked dessert is guaranteed to be popular with everyone – and it has the added bonus of being easy to make. For smart presentation, drizzle cream or yogurt over each serving and sprinkle lightly with chocolate powder.

Serves 6

200g/7oz dark (bittersweet) chocolate, chopped into small pieces

115g/4oz/½ cup unsalted (sweet) butter, plus extra for greasing

4 eggs, separated

115g/4oz/generous ½ cup caster (superfine) sugar

425g/15oz can peach slices, drained

whipped cream or Greek (US strained plain) yogurt, to serve

1 Preheat the oven to 160°C/325°F/Gas 3. Butter a wide ovenproof dish. Melt the chocolate with the butter in a heatproof bowl over barely simmering water, then remove from the heat.

2 Whisk the egg yolks with the sugar until thick and pale. In a clean, grease-free bowl, whisk the whites until stiff.

3 Beat the melted chocolate into the egg yolk mixture. Stir in a large spoonful of the egg whites, then gently fold in the remaining whites.

4 Fold the peach slices into the mixture, then turn into the prepared dish. Bake for 35–40 minutes or until risen and just firm. Serve hot, with cream or yogurt.

Variations

Pears also taste delicious with chocolate, and canned pears can be used very successfully in this recipe, instead of the peaches. During the summer months, try using very ripe peaches or a mix of soft berries instead of the canned fruit.

Peach Cobbler

A satisfying pudding in which fresh peaches are topped with a hearty almond-flavoured pastry.

Serves 6

about 1.5kg/3lb peaches, peeled and sliced

45ml/3 tbsp caster (superfine) sugar

30ml/2 tbsp peach brandy

15ml/1 tbsp freshly squeezed lemon juice

15ml/1 tbsp cornflour (cornstarch)

ice cream or crème fraîche, to serve

For the topping

115g/4oz/1 cup plain (all-purpose) flour

7.5ml/1½ tsp baking powder

1.5ml/¼ tsp salt

40g/1½oz/¼ cup finely ground almonds

50g/2oz/¼ cup caster (superfine) sugar

50g/2oz/¼ cup butter or margarine

85ml/3fl oz/⅓ cup milk

1.5ml/¼ tsp almond extract

1 Preheat the oven to 220°C/425°F/Gas 7. Place the peaches in a bowl and add the sugar, peach brandy, lemon juice and cornflour. Toss together, then spoon the peach mixture into a 2 litre/3½ pint/8 cup baking dish.

2 Now make the topping. Sift the flour, baking powder and salt into a mixing bowl. Stir in the ground almonds and all but 15ml/1 tbsp of the sugar. With two knives, or a pastry blender, cut in the butter or margarine until the mixture resembles coarse breadcrumbs.

3 Add the milk and almond extract and stir until the topping mixture is just combined.

4 Carefully drop the topping in spoonfuls on to the peaches in the baking dish. Sprinkle the top with the remaining tablespoon of caster sugar.

5 Bake for 30–35 minutes until the cobbler topping is browned. Serve hot with ice cream or crème fraîche, if you like.

Peachy Bake Energy 465Kcal/1942kJ; Protein 6.5g; Carbohydrate 48.2g, of which sugars 47.9g; Fat 28.8g, of which saturates 16.6g; Cholesterol 170mg; Calcium 47mg; Fibre 1.4g; Sodium 175mg.
Peach Cobbler Energy 299Kcal/1265kJ; Protein 4.9g; Carbohydrate 53.5g, of which sugars 36.6g; Fat 7.6g, of which saturates 4.5g; Cholesterol 19mg; Calcium 72mg; Fibre 4.4g; Sodium 62mg.

Apple Couscous Pudding

This unusual couscous mixture makes a delicious family pudding with a rich fruity flavour, but virtually no fat content. Serve with low-fat yogurt as a healthy finale to a meal.

Serves 4

600ml/1 pint/2½ cups apple juice
115g/4oz/⅔ cup couscous
40g/1½oz/scant ¼ cup sultanas (golden raisins)
2.5ml/½ tsp mixed spice
1 large cooking apple, peeled, cored and sliced
25g/1oz/2 tbsp demerara (raw) sugar
natural low-fat yogurt, to serve

1 Preheat the oven to 200°C/400°F/Gas 6. Place the apple juice, couscous, sultanas and spice in a pan and bring to the boil, stirring. Cover and simmer for 10–12 minutes, until all the free liquid is absorbed.

2 Spoon half the couscous mixture into a 1.2 litre/2 pint/5 cup ovenproof dish and top with half the apple slices. Top with the remaining couscous.

3 Arrange the remaining apple slices overlapping over the top and sprinkle with demerara sugar. Bake for 25–30 minutes, or until the apples are golden brown. Serve hot with yogurt.

> **Cook's Tip**
> Couscous is a grain product made from semolina. Normally, it is used in savoury dishes, but it makes a tasty, healthy addition to this sweet dish. The grains soften and swell on cooking.

> **Variation**
> To ring the changes, substitute other dried fruits for the sultanas in this recipe – try chopped dates or ready-to-eat apricots.

Lemon Surprise Pudding

This is a much-loved dessert many of us remember from childhood. The surprise is the unexpected sauce concealed beneath the delectable sponge.

Serves 4

50g/2oz/¼ cup butter, plus extra for greasing
grated rind and juice of 2 lemons
115g/4oz/generous ½ cup caster (superfine) sugar
2 eggs, separated
50g/2oz/½ cup self-raising (self-rising) flour
300ml/½ pint/1¼ cups milk

1 Preheat the oven to 190°C/375°F/Gas 5. Use a little butter to grease a 1.2 litre/2 pint/5 cup baking dish.

2 Beat the lemon rind, remaining butter and caster sugar in a bowl until pale and fluffy. Add the egg yolks and flour and beat together well. Gradually whisk in the lemon juice and milk (don't be alarmed if the mixture curdles horribly!).

3 In a grease-free bowl, whisk the egg whites until they form stiff peaks. Fold the egg whites lightly into the lemon mixture, then pour into the prepared baking dish.

4 Place the dish in a roasting tin (pan) and pour in hot water to come halfway up the side of the dish. Bake for about 45 minutes until golden. Serve immediately.

> **Cook's Tips**
> • The uncooked mixture may look like a curdled disaster, but as the dessert cooks it separates into a top layer of firm sponge, with a luscious lemony sauce beneath.
> • Standing the dish in a layer of water in the pan creates a gentle method of cooking – this "bain-marie" method is often used for custards and other delicate egg dishes.
> • For a slightly different accompaniment, whip thick cream with a little vanilla extract and icing (confectioners') sugar.

Apple Couscous Pudding Energy 187Kcal/797kJ; Protein 2.2g; Carbohydrate 46.4g, of which sugars 31.7g; Fat 0.5g, of which saturates 0g; Cholesterol 0mg; Calcium 26mg; Fibre 0.8g; Sodium 10mg.
Lemon Pudding Energy 319Kcal/1341kJ; Protein 7g; Carbohydrate 43.1g, of which sugars 33.8g; Fat 14.5g, of which saturates 8.1g; Cholesterol 126mg; Calcium 166mg; Fibre 0.4g; Sodium 190mg.

Spiced Red Fruit Compote

A colourful mix of succulent red fruit, delicately flavoured with aromatic spices, this dish is guaranteed to bring a touch of summer warmth to a cold day.

Serves 4
4 ripe red plums, halved
225g/8oz/2 cups strawberries, halved
225g/8oz/1⅓ cups raspberries
30ml/2 tbsp light muscovado (brown) sugar
30ml/2 tbsp water
1 cinnamon stick
3 pieces star anise
6 cloves
natural (plain) yogurt or Greek (US strained plain) yogurt, to serve

1 Place the plums, strawberries and raspberries in a heavy pan with the sugar and the water.

2 Add the cinnamon stick, star anise and cloves to the pan and heat gently, without boiling, until the sugar dissolves and the fruit juices run.

3 Cover the pan and leave the fruit to infuse over a very low heat for about 5 minutes. Remove the spices from the compote before serving warm in individual dishes, with spoonfuls of natural or Greek yogurt.

Cook's Tip
Star anise is the dried fruit of a tree native to China and is dark red-brown in colour. As its name implies, the spice is star-shaped and has an aniseed-like taste. It is quite pungent, so don't be heavy-handed with it.

Variation
Try using peaches and cherries instead of the plums and strawberries, and add a dash of liqueur for good measure.

Exotic Fruit Skewers with Lime Cheese

Lightly charred exotic fruit, served with luscious lime-flavoured cream, make the perfect finale for an *al fresco* meal. The lemon grass skewers impart a subtle lemon tang to the fruit – and look fun.

Serves 4
4 long fresh lemon grass stalks
1 mango, peeled, stoned (pitted) and cut into chunks
1 papaya, peeled, seeded and cut into chunks
1 star fruit, cut into thick slices and halved
8 fresh bay leaves
a nutmeg
60ml/4 tbsp maple syrup
50g/2oz/¼ cup demerara (raw) sugar

For the lime cheese
150g/5oz/⅔ cup curd (farmer's) cheese or low-fat soft cheese
120ml/4fl oz/½ cup double (heavy) cream
grated rind and juice of ½ lime
30ml/2 tbsp icing (confectioners') sugar

1 Prepare the barbecue or preheat the grill (broiler). Cut the top of each lemon grass stalk into a point with a sharp knife. Discard the outer leaves, then use the back of the knife to bruise the length of each stalk to release the aromatic oils. Thread each stalk, skewer-style, with a variety of the fruit pieces and bay leaves.

2 Support a piece of foil on a baking sheet and roll up the edges to make a rim. Grease the foil, lay the kebabs on top and grate a little nutmeg over each. Drizzle the maple syrup over and dust liberally with the demerara sugar. Grill (broil) for 5 minutes, until lightly charred.

3 Meanwhile, make the lime cheese. Mix together the cheese, cream, grated lime rind and juice and icing sugar in a bowl.

4 Serve the lightly charred exotic fruit kebabs along with the lime cheese.

Red Fruit Compote Energy 70Kcal/298kJ; Protein 1.5g; Carbohydrate 16.5g, of which sugars 16.5g; Fat 0.3g, of which saturates 0.1g; Cholesterol 0mg; Calcium 31mg; Fibre 2.5g; Sodium 6mg.
Exotic Fruit Energy 306Kcal/1276kJ; Protein 7.1g; Carbohydrate 28.8g, of which sugars 28.7g; Fat 19.4g, of which saturates 12g; Cholesterol 50mg; Calcium 100mg; Fibre 4.3g; Sodium 180mg.

Baked Apples with Marsala

In this recipe, the famous fortified wine from Italy – Marsala – is cooked down with the juice from the apples and the butter to make a rich, sticky sauce. For a truly indulgent dessert treat, serve up these delicious Italian-style apples with a spoonful of extra-thick cream.

Serves 6
4 medium cooking apples
50g/2oz/⅓ cup ready-to-eat dried figs
150ml/¼ pint/⅔ cup Marsala
50g/2oz/¼ cup butter, softened

1 Preheat the oven to 180°C/350°F/Gas 4. Using an apple corer, carefully remove the cores from the centre of the apples and discard.

2 Place the apples in a small, shallow baking dish and stuff the figs into the hollows of each apple.

3 Top each apple with a quarter of the butter and pour over the Marsala.

4 Cover the dish tightly with foil and bake in the preheated oven for 30 minutes.

5 Remove the foil from the apples and bake for a further 10 minutes, or until the apples are tender and the juices have reduced slightly.

6 Serve immediately with any remaining pan juices drizzled over the top.

Variation
Substitute vin santo for the Marsala for a different, but equally rich, flavour. Literally holy wine, vin santo is an intensely aromatic dessert wine from Veneto and Tuscany in Italy.

Roast Peaches with Amaretto

This lovely dish from Italy is an excellent dessert to serve in summer, when peaches are at their juiciest and most fragrant. The apricot and almond flavour of the amaretto liqueur subtly enhances the sweet, fruity taste of ripe peaches.

Serves 4
4 ripe peaches
45ml/3 tbsp Amaretto di Saronno liqueur
45ml/3 tbsp clear honey
crème fraîche or whipped cream, to serve

1 Preheat the oven to 190°C/375°F/Gas 5. Cut the peaches in half and remove the stones (pits).

2 Place the peaches, cut side up, in a roasting pan. In a small bowl, mix the amaretto liqueur with the honey, and drizzle over the halved peaches, covering them evenly.

3 Bake the peaches in the preheated oven for 20–25 minutes, or until tender. Place two peach halves on each individual plate and drizzle with the pan juices. Serve immediately with crème fraîche or whipped cream.

Cook's Tips
• If you are having difficulty removing the stones (pits), use a small sharp knife to help prise them out, but take care not to damage the peach flesh.
• You can cook these peaches over a barbecue. Place them on sheets of foil, drizzle over liqueur, then scrunch the foil around them to seal. Cook for 15–20 minutes.

Variation
Nectarines are also delicious served in this way. To ring the changes, use a different flavoured liqueur – orange liqueur, such as Grand Marnier, would work well.

Baked Apples Energy 134Kcal/560kJ; Protein 0.5g; Carbohydrate 11.1g, of which sugars 11.1g; Fat 7g, of which saturates 4.3g; Cholesterol 18mg; Calcium 24mg; Fibre 1.3g; Sodium 57mg.
Roast Peaches Energy 98Kcal/418kJ; Protein 1.2g; Carbohydrate 20.7g, of which sugars 20.7g; Fat 0.1g, of which saturates 0g; Cholesterol 0mg; Calcium 9mg; Fibre 1.7g; Sodium 4mg.

Papaya Baked with Ginger

For a dessert with a difference, why not serve this hot papaya dish? Ginger enhances the flavour of the fruit while the nuts provide a crunchy contrast to the creamy, orange flesh.

Serves 4
2 ripe papayas
2 pieces preserved stem ginger in syrup, drained, plus 15ml/ 1 tbsp syrup from the jar

8 amaretti or other dessert biscuits (cookies), coarsely crushed
45ml/3 tbsp raisins
shredded, finely pared rind and juice of 1 lime
25g/1oz/¼ cup pistachio nuts, chopped
15ml/1 tbsp light muscovado (brown) sugar
60ml/4 tbsp crème fraîche, plus extra to serve

1 Preheat the oven to 200°C/400°F/Gas 6. Cut the papayas in half and scoop out their seeds. Place the halves in a baking dish and set aside. Cut the stem ginger into fine matchsticks.

2 Make the filling. Combine the crushed amaretti, stem ginger matchsticks and raisins in a bowl.

3 Stir in the lime rind and juice, two thirds of the nuts, then add the sugar and the crème fraîche. Mix well.

4 Fill the papaya halves and drizzle with the ginger syrup. Sprinkle with the remaining nuts. Bake for about 25 minutes or until tender. Serve with extra crème fraîche.

> **Variation**
> *Use Greek (US strained plain) yogurt and toasted almonds instead of crème fraîche and pistachios.*

> **Cook's Tip**
> *Don't overcook papaya or the flesh will turn watery.*

Tropical Fruit Gratin

This out-of-the-ordinary gratin is strictly for grown-ups. A colourful combination of fruit is topped with a simple sabayon before being quickly browned.

Serves 4
2 tamarillos
½ sweet pineapple
1 ripe mango
175g/6oz/1½ cups blackberries
120ml/4fl oz/½ cup sparkling white wine
115g/4oz/generous ½ cup caster (superfine) sugar
6 egg yolks

1 Cut each tamarillo in half lengthways and then into thick slices. Cut the rind and core from the pineapple and take spiral slices off the outside to remove the eyes. Cut the flesh into chunks. Peel the mango, cut it in half and cut the flesh from the stone (pit) in slices.

2 Divide all the fruit, including the blackberries, among four 14cm/5½in gratin dishes placed on a baking sheet and set aside. Heat the wine and sugar in a pan until the sugar has dissolved. Bring to the boil and cook for 5 minutes.

3 Put the egg yolks in a large heatproof bowl. Place the bowl over a pan of simmering water and whisk until pale. Slowly pour on the hot sugar syrup, whisking all the time, until the mixture thickens. Preheat the grill (broiler).

4 Spoon the mixture over the fruit. Place the baking sheet holding the dishes on a low shelf under the hot grill until the topping is golden. Serve hot.

> **Variation**
> *Although boiling drives off the alcohol in the wine, children do not always appreciate the flavour, so substitute orange juice if making the gratin for them. White grape juice or pineapple juice would also work well.*

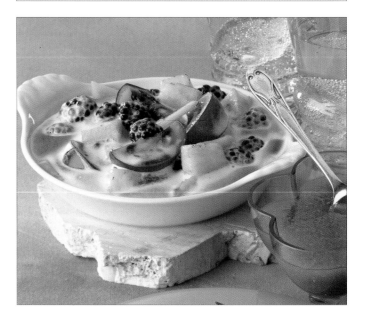

Papaya with Ginger Energy 285Kcal/1197kJ; Protein 3.5g; Carbohydrate 45.5g, of which sugars 40.9g; Fat 11.1g, of which saturates 5.1g; Cholesterol 17mg; Calcium 94mg; Fibre 6.3g; Sodium 99mg.
Tropical Fruit Gratin Energy 313Kcal/1322kJ; Protein 6.2g; Carbohydrate 51.5g, of which sugars 51.4g; Fat 8.8g, of which saturates 2.5g; Cholesterol 302mg; Calcium 99mg; Fibre 4.3g; Sodium 27mg.

Warm Autumn Compote

An unusual combination of pears, figs and raspberries.

Serves 4

75g/3oz/6 tbsp caster (superfine) sugar
1 bottle red wine
1 vanilla pod (bean), split
1 strip pared lemon rind
4 pears
2 purple figs, quartered
225g/8oz/1⅓ cups raspberries
freshly squeezed lemon juice, to taste

1 Put the sugar and wine in a large pan and heat gently until the sugar has dissolved. Add the vanilla pod and lemon rind and bring to the boil, then simmer for 5 minutes.

2 Peel and halve the pears, then scoop out the cores, using a melon baller or a teaspoon. Add the pears to the syrup and poach for 15 minutes, carefully turning the pears several times so that they colour evenly. Add the figs to the pan and poach for a further 5 minutes, until the fruits are tender.

3 Transfer the poached pears and figs to a serving bowl using a slotted spoon, then sprinkle over the raspberries.

4 Return the syrup to the heat and boil rapidly to reduce slightly and concentrate the flavour. Add a little lemon juice to taste. Strain the syrup over the fruits and serve warm.

Variation/Cherry Compote
Combine 120ml/4fl oz/½ cup red wine, 50g/2oz/¼ cup light muscovado (brown) sugar, 50g/2oz/¼ cup granulated sugar, 15ml/1 tbsp honey, two 2.5cm/1in strips of pared orange rind and 1.5ml/¼ tsp almond extract in a pan with 120ml/4fl oz/½ cup water. Stir over medium heat until the sugar dissolves, then increase the heat and boil until the liquid reduces slightly. Add 675g/1½lb pitted sweet fresh cherries and bring back to the boil, skimming off any foam. Reduce the heat slightly and simmer for 8–10 minutes. Serve lukewarm on ice cream.

Cherries Jubilee

Fresh black or red cherries taste wonderful cooked lightly and served hot over ice cream. A great idea for a mid-week meal when time is short.

Serves 4

450g/1lb sweet fresh cherries
115g/4oz/generous ½ cup caster (superfine) sugar
pared rind of 1 lemon
300ml/½ pint/1¼ cups water, plus 15ml/1 tbsp
15ml/1 tbsp arrowroot
60ml/4 tbsp Kirsch
vanilla ice cream, to serve

1 Pit the cherries over a pan to catch the juice. Drop the pits into the pan as you work.

2 Add the sugar, lemon rind and 300ml/½ pint/1¼ cups water to the pan. Stir over a low heat until the sugar has dissolved, then bring to the boil and simmer for 10 minutes. Strain the syrup, then return to the pan. Add the cherries and cook for 3–4 minutes. Remove from the heat.

3 Blend the arrowroot to a paste with 15ml/1 tbsp cold water and stir into the cherries.

4 Return the pan to the heat. Bring to the boil, stirring all the time. Cook the sauce for a minute or two, stirring until thick and smooth.

5 Heat the Kirsch in a ladle over a flame, ignite and pour over the cherries. Spoon the cherries and hot sauce over scoops of ice cream and serve immediately.

Cook's Tips
• If you don't have a cherry pitter, simply push the pits through with a skewer, keeping the fruit whole. Remember to do this over a pan (or plate), so that you can catch the juice.
• When buying fresh cherries, look for well-coloured fruits and avoid any that are split, as they will be over-ripe.

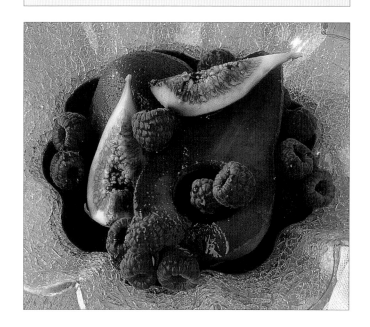

Cherries Jubilee Energy 206Kcal/873kJ; Protein 1.2g; Carbohydrate 47.9g, of which sugars 47.9g; Fat 0.1g, of which saturates 0g; Cholesterol 0mg; Calcium 30mg; Fibre 1g; Sodium 3mg.
Autumn Compote Energy 298Kcal/1257kJ; Protein 1.9g; Carbohydrate 42.9g, of which sugars 42.9g; Fat 0.5g, of which saturates 0.1g; Cholesterol 0mg; Calcium 79mg; Fibre 5.5g; Sodium 27mg.

Stuffed Peaches with Mascarpone Cream

Peaches with an almond-flavoured filling and topped with a rich cream make a delicious Italian-style dessert for summer entertaining.

Serves 4

4 large peaches, halved and stoned (pitted)
40g/1½oz amaretti, crumbled
30ml/2 tbsp ground almonds
45ml/3 tbsp sugar
15ml/1 tbsp cocoa powder (unsweetened)

150ml/¼ pint/⅔ cup sweet white wine
25g/1oz/2 tbsp butter

For the mascarpone cream
25g/1oz/2 tbsp caster (superfine) sugar
3 egg yolks
15ml/1 tbsp sweet white wine
225g/8oz/1 cup mascarpone
150ml/¼ pint/⅔ cup double (heavy) cream

1 Preheat the oven to 200°C/400°F/Gas 6. Using a teaspoon, scoop some of the flesh from the cavities in the peaches, to make a reasonable space for the stuffing. Chop the scooped-out flesh.

2 Mix together the amaretti, ground almonds, sugar, cocoa and peach flesh. Now add enough wine to make the mixture into a thick paste.

3 Place the peaches in a buttered ovenproof dish and fill them with the stuffing. Dot with the butter, then pour the remaining wine into the dish. Bake in the oven for 35 minutes.

4 Make the mascarpone cream. Beat the sugar and egg yolks until thick and pale. Stir in the wine, then fold in the mascarpone. Whip the double cream to form soft peaks and fold into the mixture.

5 Remove the stuffed peaches from the oven and leave to cool slightly. Serve the peaches still warm, along with the mascarpone cream.

Baked Lattice Peaches

Nectarines also work well in this lovely recipe.

Serves 6

3 peaches
juice of ½ lemon
75g/3oz/scant ½ cup white marzipan
375g/13oz ready-rolled puff pastry
a large pinch of ground cinnamon

beaten egg, to glaze
caster (superfine) sugar, for sprinkling

For the caramel sauce
50g/2oz/¼ cup caster (superfine) sugar
30ml/2 tbsp water
150ml/¼ pint/⅔ cup double (heavy) cream

1 Preheat the oven to 190°C/375°F/Gas 5. Pour boiling water over the peaches to cover. Leave for 60 seconds, then drain and peel. Toss the fruit in the lemon juice to prevent browning.

2 Divide the marzipan into six pieces and shape each to form a small round. Cut the peaches in half and remove their stones (pits). Fill the cavity in each peach with a marzipan round.

3 Unroll the puff pastry and cut in half. Set one half aside, then cut out six rounds from the rest, making each one slightly larger than a peach half. Sprinkle a little cinnamon on each pastry round, then place a peach half, marzipan-side down, on top.

4 Cut the remaining pastry into lattice pastry, using a special cutter if you have one. If not, simply cut small slits in rows all over the pastry. Cut the lattice pastry into six equal squares.

5 Dampen the edges of the pastry rounds with water, then drape a lattice pastry square over each peach half. Press the pastry edges to seal, then trim and decorate with pastry leaves made from the trimmings. Transfer to a baking sheet. Brush with beaten egg, sprinkle with sugar and bake for 20 minutes.

6 Meanwhile, make the sauce. Heat the sugar with the water in a small pan until it dissolves. Boil until the syrup turns dark golden. Stand back and add the cream. Heat gently, stirring until smooth. Serve the peach pastries with the sauce.

Stuffed Peaches Energy 641Kcal/2670kJ; Protein 12.7g; Carbohydrate 40.9g, of which sugars 36g; Fat 45.3g, of which saturates 23.9g; Cholesterol 290mg; Calcium 102mg; Fibre 2.7g; Sodium 132mg.
Lattice Peaches Energy 452Kcal/1886kJ; Protein 5.1g; Carbohydrate 43.8g, of which sugars 21.4g; Fat 30.4g, of which saturates 8.5g; Cholesterol 34mg; Calcium 64mg; Fibre 0.8g; Sodium 203mg.

Hot Bananas with Rum & Raisins

A classic way of serving bananas, the rum is set alight just before serving. This gives the fruit a wonderful, distinctive flavour, making an irresistible dish.

Serves 4

40g/1½oz/scant ¼ cup seedless raisins
75ml/5 tbsp dark rum
50g/2oz/¼ cup unsalted (sweet) butter
60ml/4 tbsp soft light brown sugar
4 ripe bananas, peeled and halved lengthways
1.5ml/¼ tsp grated nutmeg
1.5ml/¼ tsp ground cinnamon
30ml/2 tbsp slivered almonds, toasted
chilled cream or vanilla ice cream, to serve (optional)

1 Put the raisins in a bowl with the rum. Leave them to soak for about 30 minutes to plump up.

2 Melt the butter in a frying pan, add the sugar and stir until the sugar has dissolved. Add the bananas and cook for a few minutes until they are tender.

3 Sprinkle the nutmeg and cinnamon over the bananas, then pour in the rum and raisins. Carefully set alight using a long taper and stir gently to mix.

4 Scatter with the almonds and serve immediately with chilled cream or vanilla ice cream, if you like.

Cook's Tips
• Choose almost-ripe bananas with evenly coloured skins, either all yellow or just green at the tips. Over-ripe bananas will not hold their shape so well when cooked.
• Setting light to the rum, known as flambéeing, dispels most of the alcohol content but imparts to the bananas an intense flavour. You must, of course, take great care when lighting the rum and it is essential that you use a long taper.

Apple Fritters

Make sure you buy plenty of apples for this recipe. The fritters taste so good you'll probably have to cook an extra batch. The fritters are delicious eaten on their own, but you could serve them with a sprinkling of lemon juice or natural (plain) yogurt for a tangy finish.

Serves 4–6

130g/4½oz/generous 1 cup plain (all-purpose) flour
10ml/2 tsp baking powder
1.5ml/¼ tsp salt
150ml/¼ pint/⅔ cup milk
1 egg, beaten
vegetable oil, for deep-frying
150g/5oz/¾ cup granulated sugar
5ml/1 tsp ground cinnamon
2 large tart eating apples, peeled, cored and cut in 5mm/¼in slices
icing sugar, for dusting

1 Sift the flour, baking powder and salt into a bowl. Beat in the milk and egg with a wire whisk.

2 Place at least 7.5cm/3in of oil in a heavy frying pan and heat to 185°C/360°F or until a cube of bread dropped into the oil turns brown in 1–2 minutes.

3 Mix the granulated sugar and cinnamon in a shallow bowl or plate. Toss the apple slices in the sugar mixture to coat all over.

4 Dip the apple slices in the batter, using a fork or slotted spoon. Drain off the excess batter. Fry, in batches, in the hot oil for 4–5 minutes, until golden brown on both sides. Drain the fritters on kitchen paper and keep warm.

5 Place the icing sugar in a sieve (strainer) and sprinkle over the fritters, tapping the side of the sieve with your hand. Serve hot.

Variation
Use 2 or 3 medium pears, sliced, in place of the apples.

Hot Bananas Energy 362Kcal/1516kJ; Protein 3.2g; Carbohydrate 46.4g, of which sugars 43.9g; Fat 14.8g, of which saturates 7g; Cholesterol 27mg; Calcium 39mg; Fibre 1.9g; Sodium 85mg.
Apple Fritters Energy 303Kcal/1275kJ; Protein 4.1g; Carbohydrate 46.1g, of which sugars 29.6g; Fat 12.7g, of which saturates 1.9g; Cholesterol 33mg; Calcium 79mg; Fibre 1g; Sodium 25mg.

Golden Pineapple with Papaya Sauce

Pineapple cooked in this way takes on a superb flavour and is sensational when served with the papaya sauce.

Serves 6
1 sweet pineapple
melted butter, for greasing and brushing
2 pieces drained, preserved stem ginger in syrup, cut into fine matchsticks, plus 30ml/2 tbsp of the syrup from the jar
30ml/2 tbsp demerara (raw) sugar
pinch of ground cinnamon
fresh mint sprigs, to decorate

For the sauce
1 ripe papaya, peeled and seeded
175ml/6fl oz/¾ cup apple juice

1 Peel the pineapple and take spiral slices off the outside to remove the eyes. Cut the flesh crossways into six slices, each 2.5cm/1in thick. Line a baking sheet with a sheet of foil, rolling up the sides to make a rim. Grease the foil with melted butter. Preheat the grill (broiler).

2 Arrange the pineapple slices on the lined baking sheet. Brush with melted butter, then top with the ginger matchsticks, sugar and cinnamon. Drizzle over the stem ginger syrup. Grill (broil) for 5–7 minutes or until the slices are golden and lightly charred on top.

3 Meanwhile, make the sauce. Cut a few slices from the papaya and set aside, then purée the rest with the apple juice in a blender or food processor.

4 Press the purée through a sieve (strainer) placed over a bowl, then stir in any juices from cooking the pineapple. Serve the pineapple slices with a little sauce drizzled around each plate. Decorate with the reserved papaya slices and the mint sprigs.

> **Cook's Tip**
> Try the papaya sauce with savoury dishes, too. It tastes great with grilled chicken and game birds as well as pork and lamb.

Thai Fried Pineapple

A very simple and quick Thai dessert – the pineapple is fried in butter, brown sugar and lime juice, then sprinkled with toasted coconut. The slightly sharp taste of the fruit makes this a very refreshing treat at the end of a meal.

Serves 4
1 pineapple
40g/1½oz/3 tbsp butter
15ml/1 tbsp desiccated (dry unsweetened shredded) coconut
60ml/4 tbsp soft light brown sugar
60ml/4 tbsp freshly squeezed lime juice
lime slices or quarters, to decorate
thick and creamy natural (plain) yogurt, to serve

1 Using a sharp knife, cut the top off the pineapple and peel off the skin, taking care to remove the eyes as you work around the fruit. Cut the pineapple in half lengthways, and cut out and discard the woody core. Then slice the flesh lengthways into 1cm-/½in-wide wedges.

2 Heat the butter in a large, heavy frying pan or wok. When it has melted, add the pineapple wedges and cook over a medium heat for 1–2 minutes on each side, or until they have turned pale golden in colour.

3 Meanwhile, dry-fry the coconut in a small frying pan until lightly browned, shaking the pan frequently to cook evenly. Remove from the heat and set aside.

4 Sprinkle the sugar into the pan with the pineapple, add the lime juice and cook, stirring constantly, until the sugar has completely dissolved.

5 Divide the pineapple wedges and cooking juices among four individual bowls. Sprinkle each serving with some of the fried coconut, decorate with the lime slices and serve immediately with the natural yogurt.

Golden Pineapple Energy 130Kcal/558kJ; Protein 1g; Carbohydrate 32.9g, of which sugars 32.9g; Fat 0.4g, of which saturates 0g; Cholesterol 0mg; Calcium 49mg; Fibre 3.4g; Sodium 21mg.
Thai Pineapple Energy 238Kcal/1004kJ; Protein 1.2g; Carbohydrate 36.2g, of which sugars 36.2g; Fat 11g, of which saturates 7.2g; Cholesterol 21mg; Calcium 47mg; Fibre 2.9g; Sodium 67mg.

Fried Bananas

A favourite with children and adults alike, these delicious banana treats are particularly popular in South-east Asia.

Serves 4

115g/4oz/1 cup plain
  (all-purpose) flour
2.5ml/½ tsp bicarbonate of soda
  (baking soda)
pinch of salt
30ml/2 tbsp granulated sugar
1 egg, beaten
90ml/6 tbsp water
30ml/2 tbsp desiccated (dry
  unsweetened shredded)
  coconut or 15ml/1 tbsp
  sesame seeds
4 firm bananas
vegetable oil, for deep-frying
fresh mint sprigs, to decorate
30ml/2 tbsp clear honey, to serve
  (optional)

1 Sift the flour, bicarbonate of soda and salt into a large bowl. Stir in the granulated sugar and the egg, and whisk in just enough of the water to make quite a thin batter.

2 Whisk the coconut or sesame seeds into the batter so that they are evenly distributed.

3 Peel the bananas. Carefully cut each one in half lengthways, then in half crossways to make 16 pieces of about the same size. Don't do this until you are ready to cook because, once peeled, bananas quickly discolour.

4 Heat the oil in a wok or deep-fryer to a temperature of 190°C/375°F or until a cube of bread dropped into the oil browns in about 45 seconds. Dip the banana pieces in the batter, then gently drop a few into the oil. Deep-fry until golden brown, then lift out and drain well on kitchen paper.

5 Cook the remaining banana pieces in the same way. Serve immediately with honey, if using, and decorated with mint.

> **Variation**
> This recipe works well with pineapple rings or apple wedges.

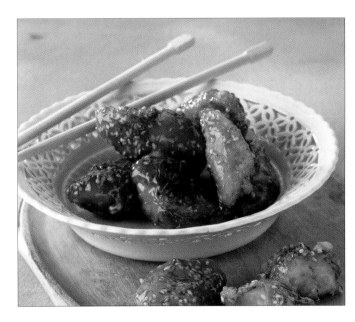

Toffee Bananas

Work quickly when dipping the fruit in the caramel, as it will cool and set quickly.

Serves 4

4 firm bananas
75g/3oz/⅔ cup plain
  (all-purpose) flour
50g/2oz/½ cup cornflour
  (cornstarch)
10ml/2 tsp baking powder
175ml/6fl oz/¾ cup water
5ml/1 tsp sesame oil
groundnut (peanut), sunflower or
  corn oil, for deep-frying

For the caramel
200g/7oz/1 cup granulated sugar
30ml/2 tbsp sesame seeds
60ml/4 tbsp water

1 Peel the bananas, then cut them diagonally into thick slices. Sift the flours and baking powder into a large bowl. Quickly beat in the water and sesame oil, taking care not to overmix. Stir in the bananas until coated.

2 Heat the oil in a deep pan to a temperature of 180°C/350°F or until a cube of bread turns pale brown in 45 seconds.

3 Using a fork, remove a piece of banana from the batter, allowing the excess batter to drain off. Gently lower the coated piece into the hot oil. Add more pieces but do not overcrowd the pan. Fry for about 2 minutes or until the coating is golden.

4 Remove the cooked fritters from the oil with a slotted spoon and drain on kitchen paper. Cook the rest in the same way.

5 When all the banana pieces have been fried, make the caramel. Mix the sugar, sesame seeds and water in a pan. Heat gently, stirring occasionally, until the sugar has dissolved. Increase the heat slightly and continue cooking, without stirring, until the syrup becomes a light caramel. Remove from the heat.

6 Have ready a bowl of iced water. Working quickly, drop one fritter at a time into the hot caramel. Flip over with a fork, remove immediately and plunge into the iced water. Remove from the water quickly (using your fingers for speed, but taking care) and drain on a wire rack while coating the rest.

Fried Bananas Energy 385Kcal/1616kJ; Protein 5.9g; Carbohydrate 53.9g, of which sugars 29.7g; Fat 17.7g, of which saturates 5.8g; Cholesterol 48mg; Calcium 59mg; Fibre 3g; Sodium 22mg.
Toffee Bananas Energy 551Kcal/2324kJ; Protein 4.7g; Carbohydrate 101.6g, of which sugars 73.5g; Fat 16.7g, of which saturates 2.2g; Cholesterol 0mg; Calcium 111mg; Fibre 2.3g; Sodium 13mg.

Tropical Fruit with Maple Butter

This dish turns exotic fruit into comfort food.

Serves 4
1 large mango
1 large papaya
1 small pineapple
2 bananas
115g/4oz/½ cup unsalted (sweet) butter
60ml/4 tbsp maple syrup
ground cinnamon, for sprinkling

1 Peel the mango and cut the flesh into large pieces. Halve the papaya and scoop out the seeds. Cut into thick slices, then peel. Peel and core the pineapple and slice into thin wedges. Peel the bananas, then halve them lengthways.

2 Cut the butter into small dice and place in a blender or food processor with the maple syrup, then process until creamy.

3 Place the mango, papaya, pineapple and banana on a grill (broiler) rack and brush with the maple syrup butter. Cook under a medium heat for about 10 minutes, until just tender, turning the fruit occasionally and brushing it with the butter.

4 Arrange the fruit on a serving platter and dot with the remaining butter. Sprinkle over a little cinnamon and serve hot.

Variation/Tropical Fruits in Cinnamon Syrup
Sprinkle a third of 450g/1lb/2¼ cups caster (superfine) sugar over the base of a large pan. Add 1 cinnamon stick and half of the following: about 675g/1½lb papayas, peeled, seeded and cut into thin pieces; about 675g/1½lb mangoes, peeled, stoned (pitted) and cut lengthways into thin pieces; about 225g/8oz star fruit, thinly sliced. Sprinkle half the remaining sugar over the fruit pieces. Add the remaining fruit, sprinkled with the remaining sugar. Cover and cook over a medium-low heat for 35–45 minutes, until the sugar melts. Shake the pan occasionally, but do not stir (the fruit will collapse). Simmer, uncovered, for 10 minutes, until the fruit is becoming translucent. Remove from the heat and cool. Transfer to a bowl and chill, covered, overnight. Serve with yogurt or crème fraîche.

Blueberry Pancakes

These are rather like the thick American breakfast pancakes – though they can, of course, be eaten at any time of the day.

Makes 6–8
115g/4oz/1 cup self-raising (self-rising) flour
pinch of salt
45–60ml/3–4 tbsp caster (superfine) sugar
2 eggs
120ml/4fl oz/½ cup milk
15–30ml/1–2 tbsp oil
115g/4oz/1 cup fresh or frozen blueberries, plus extra to decorate
maple syrup, to serve
lemon wedges, to decorate

1 Sift the flour into a bowl with the salt and sugar. Beat together the eggs thoroughly. Make a well in the middle of the flour and stir in the eggs.

2 Gradually blend in a little of the milk to make a smooth batter. Then whisk in the rest of the milk and whisk for 1–2 minutes. Allow to rest for 20–30 minutes.

3 Heat a few drops of oil in a pancake pan or heavy frying pan until just hazy. Pour about 30ml/2 tbsp of the batter and swirl the batter around until it makes an even shape.

4 Cook for 2–3 minutes and when almost set on top, sprinkle over 15–30ml/1–2 tbsp blueberries. As soon as the base is loose and golden brown, turn the pancake over.

5 Cook on the second side for only about 1 minute, until golden and crisp. Slide the pancake on to a plate and serve drizzled with maple syrup. Continue with the rest of the batter. Serve decorated with lemon wedges and a few extra blueberries.

Cook's Tip
Instead of blueberries you could use blackberries or raspberries. If you use canned fruit, make sure it is very well drained.

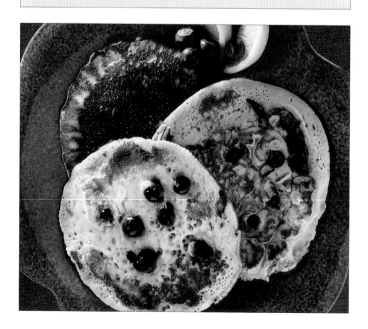

Tropical Fruit Energy 470Kcal/1974kJ; Protein 2.7g; Carbohydrate 64g, of which sugars 62.7g; Fat 24.4g, of which saturates 15.1g; Cholesterol 61mg; Calcium 90mg; Fibre 7.7g; Sodium 229mg.
Blueberry Pancakes Energy 111Kcal/468kJ; Protein 3.5g; Carbohydrate 18.2g, of which sugars 7.5g; Fat 3.2g, of which saturates 0.8g; Cholesterol 48mg; Calcium 84mg; Fibre 0.9g; Sodium 76mg.

Rhubarb-Strawberry Crisp

Strawberries, cinnamon and ground almonds make this a luxurious and delicious version of rhubarb crumble that's sure to go down well with all the family.

Serves 4
225g/8oz strawberries, hulled
450g/1lb rhubarb, diced
90g/3½oz/½ cup granulated
  sugar
15ml/1 tbsp cornflour
  (cornstarch)

85ml/3fl oz/⅓ cup fresh
  orange juice
115g/4oz/1 cup plain (all-
  purpose) flour
90g/3½oz/1 cup rolled oats
115g/4oz/½ cup light muscovado
  (brown) sugar
2.5ml/½ tsp ground cinnamon
50g/2oz/½ cup ground
  almonds
150g/5oz/10 tbsp cold butter
1 egg, lightly beaten
single (light) cream or natural
  (plain) yogurt, to serve

1 If the strawberries are large, cut them in half. Combine the strawberries, rhubarb and granulated sugar in a 2.4 litre/4 pint/10 cup baking dish. Preheat the oven to 180°C/350°F/Gas 4.

2 In a small bowl, blend the cornflour with the orange juice. Pour this mixture over the fruit and stir gently to coat. Set the baking dish aside while making the crumble topping.

3 In a bowl, toss together the flour, oats, muscovado sugar, cinnamon and ground almonds. With a pastry blender or two knives, cut in the butter until the mixture resembles coarse breadcrumbs. Stir in the beaten egg.

4 Spoon the oat mixture evenly over the fruit and press down gently. Cook in the oven for 50–60 minutes, until the top is golden brown. Serve warm with single cream or yogurt.

> **Cook's Tip**
> *Rolled oats and ground almonds not only add interesting texture to the topping, but also turn this dish into a healthier version of traditional crumble.*

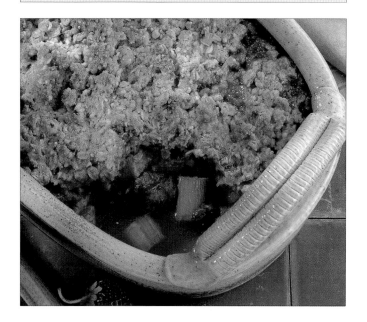

Apple Soufflé Omelette

Apples sautéed until they are slightly caramelized make a delicious autumn filling for these light-as-air sweet pancakes. Great for an impromptu supper.

Serves 2
4 eggs, separated
30ml/2 tbsp single (light) cream
15ml/1 tbsp caster
  (superfine) sugar

15g/½oz/1 tbsp butter
icing (confectioners') sugar, for
  dredging

For the filling
1 eating apple, peeled, cored
  and sliced
25g/1oz/2 tbsp butter
30ml/2 tbsp soft light brown
  sugar
45ml/3 tbsp single (light) cream

1 Make the filling. Sauté the apple slices in the butter and sugar until just tender. Stir in the cream and keep warm while making the omelette.

2 Place the egg yolks in a bowl with the cream and sugar and beat well. Whisk the egg whites until they form stiff peaks, then fold into the yolk mixture.

3 Melt the butter in a large heavy frying pan, pour in the soufflé mixture and spread evenly. Cook for 1 minute until golden underneath, then cover the pan handle with foil and place under a hot grill (broiler) to brown the top.

4 Slide the omelette on to a plate, add the apple mixture, then fold over. Sift the icing sugar over thickly, then mark in a criss-cross pattern with a hot metal skewer. Serve immediately.

> **Cook's Tips**
> *• When cooking the top, remove the omelette as soon as it is browned. Do not overcook at this stage otherwise the light texture of the omelette will be damaged.*
> *• Try replacing the apples with fresh raspberries or strawberries when they are in season.*

Apple Omelette Energy 469Kcal/1952kJ; Protein 14.1g; Carbohydrate 27.5g, of which sugars 27.5g; Fat 34.8g, of which saturates 18.1g; Cholesterol 444mg; Calcium 107mg; Fibre 0.6g; Sodium 274mg.
Rh.-Strawb. Crisp Energy 808Kcal/3390kJ; Protein 11.8g; Carbohydrate 103g, of which sugars 60.9g; Fat 41.7g, of which saturates 20.5g; Cholesterol 128mg; Calcium 240mg; Fibre 5.6g; Sodium 269mg.

Apple Charlottes

These tempting little fruit Charlottes are a wonderful way to use windfalls.

Serves 4
175g/6oz/¾ cup butter
450g/1lb cooking apples
225g/8oz eating apples
60ml/4 tbsp water

130g/4½oz/scant ⅔ cup caster (superfine) sugar
2 egg yolks
pinch of grated nutmeg
9 thin slices white bread, crusts removed
extra-thick double (heavy) cream or custard, to serve

1 Preheat the oven to 190°C/375°F/Gas 5. Put a knob (pat) of the butter in a pan. Peel and core the apples, dice them finely and put them in the pan with the water. Cover and cook for 10 minutes or until the cooking apples have pulped down. Stir in 115g/4oz/½ cup of the caster sugar. Boil, uncovered, until any liquid has evaporated and what remains is a thick pulp. Remove from the heat, beat in the egg yolks and nutmeg and set aside.

2 Melt the remaining butter in a separate pan over a low heat until the white curds start to separate from the clear yellow liquid. Remove from the heat. Leave to stand for a few minutes, then strain the clear clarified butter through a sieve (strainer) lined with muslin (cheesecloth), discarding the curds.

3 Brush four 150ml/¼ pint/⅔ cup individual Charlotte moulds or round tins (pans) with a little of the clarified butter; sprinkle with the remaining caster sugar. Cut the bread slices into 2.5cm/1in strips. Dip the strips into the remaining clarified butter; use to line the moulds or tins. Overlap the strips on the base to give the effect of a swirl and let the excess bread overhang the tops of the moulds or tins.

4 Fill each bread case with apple pulp. Fold the excess bread over the top of each mould or tin to make a lid and press down lightly. Bake for 45–50 minutes or until golden. Run a knife between each Charlotte and its mould or tin, then turn out on to dessert plates. Serve immediately with extra-thick double cream or custard.

Rhubarb Spiral Cobbler

Orange in the fruit filling and in the topping gives this pudding added zest.

Serves 4
675g/1½lb rhubarb, sliced
50g/2oz/¼ cup caster (superfine) sugar
45ml/3 tbsp orange juice

For the topping
200g/7oz/1¾ cups self-raising (self-rising) flour

30ml/2 tbsp caster (superfine) sugar
about 200g/7oz/scant 1 cup natural (plain) yogurt
grated rind of 1 medium orange
30ml/2 tbsp demerara (raw) sugar
5ml/1 tsp ground ginger
yogurt or fresh ready-made custard, to serve

1 Preheat the oven to 200°C/400°F/Gas 6. Cook the rhubarb, sugar and orange juice in a covered pan until tender. Transfer to an ovenproof dish.

2 Make the topping. Put the flour in a mixing bowl, add the caster sugar and mix together. Stir in enough of the yogurt to bind to a soft dough.

3 Roll out on a floured surface to a 25cm/10in square. Mix together the orange rind, demerara sugar and ginger in a bowl, then sprinkle the mixture evenly over the surface of the dough.

4 Roll up quite tightly, then cut into about ten slices, using a sharp knife. Arrange the slices over the rhubarb.

5 Bake in the oven for 15–20 minutes, or until the spirals are well risen and golden brown. Serve warm, with yogurt or fresh custard.

> **Variation**
> For a cinnamon cobbler topping, leave out the orange rind and replace the ginger with ground cinnamon.

Apple Charlottes Energy 686Kcal/2874kJ; Protein 7.5g; Carbohydrate 79.2g, of which sugars 50.8g; Fat 40g, of which saturates 23.6g; Cholesterol 194mg; Calcium 111mg; Fibre 3.6g; Sodium 591mg.
Rhubarb Cobbler Energy 317Kcal/1355kJ; Protein 8.7g; Carbohydrate 72.6g, of which sugars 35.5g; Fat 1.3g, of which saturates 0.4g; Cholesterol 1mg; Calcium 443mg; Fibre 3.9g; Sodium 229mg.

Blackberry Cobbler

Make the most of the fresh autumn blackberries with this delicious dessert. Break through the scrumptious topping to reveal the dark, juicy fruit. Serve with whipped cream for a truly satisfying dish to herald in a new season.

Serves 8
800g/1¾lb/6 cups blackberries
200g/7oz/1 cup granulated sugar
20g/¾oz/scant ¼ cup plain (all-purpose) flour
grated rind of 1 lemon
30ml/2 tbsp granulated sugar mixed with 1.5ml/¼ tsp grated nutmeg

For the topping
225g/8oz/2 cups plain (all-purpose) flour
200g/7oz/1 cup granulated sugar
15ml/1 tbsp baking powder
pinch of salt
250ml/8fl oz/1 cup milk
115g/4oz/½ cup butter, melted

1 Preheat the oven to 180°C/350°F/Gas 4. In a bowl, combine the blackberries, sugar, flour and lemon rind. Stir gently to blend. Transfer to a 2.4 litre/4 pint/10 cup baking dish.

2 Make the topping. Sift the flour, sugar, baking powder and salt into a large bowl. Combine the milk and butter in a jug (pitcher).

3 Gradually stir the milk mixture into the dry ingredients and stir until the batter is just smooth.

4 Spoon the batter over the berries, levelling the top and spreading to the edges.

5 Sprinkle the surface with the sugar and nutmeg mixture. Bake for about 50 minutes, until the topping is set and lightly browned. Serve immediately.

> **Cook's Tip**
> Use half blackberries and half raspberries or tayberries for the filling, to ring the changes.

Black Cherry Clafoutis

This favourite French recipe has been reproduced with all manner of fruit, but you simply can't beat the classic version using slightly tart black cherries.

Serves 6
25g/1oz/2 tbsp butter, for greasing
450g/1lb/generous 2 cups black cherries, pitted
25g/1oz/¼ cup plain (all-purpose) flour
50g/2oz/½ cup icing (confectioners') sugar, plus extra for dusting
4 eggs, beaten
250ml/8fl oz/1 cup full cream (whole) milk
30ml/2 tbsp Kirsch

1 Preheat the oven to 180°C/350°F/Gas 4. Use the butter to thickly grease a 1.2 litre/2 pint/5 cup ovenproof dish. Sprinkle the cherries over the base.

2 Sift the flour and icing sugar together into a large mixing bowl and gradually whisk in the eggs until the mixture is smooth. Whisk in the milk until blended, then stir in the Kirsch.

3 Pour the batter carefully over the cherries, then bake for 35–45 minutes or until just set and lightly golden.

4 Allow the pudding to cool for about 15 minutes. Dust liberally with icing sugar just before serving.

> **Cook's Tip**
> Traditionally, the pits are left in the cherries, but removing them first makes the dish easier to eat.

> **Variations**
> Try other liqueurs in this dessert. Almond-flavoured liqueur is delicious teamed with cherries, as is raspberry or orange liqueur.

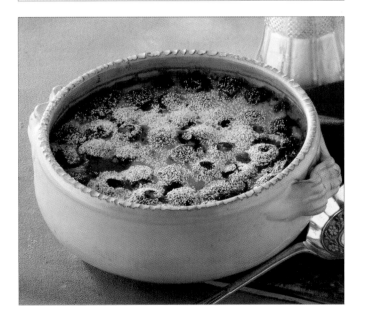

Blackberry Cobbler Energy 463Kcal/1952kJ; Protein 5.2g; Carbohydrate 86.6g, of which sugars 63.3g; Fat 13g, of which saturates 7.9g; Cholesterol 32mg; Calcium 153mg; Fibre 4.1g; Sodium 107mg.
Cherry Clafoutis Energy 201Kcal/843kJ; Protein 6.7g; Carbohydrate 23.8g, of which sugars 20.7g; Fat 8.9g, of which saturates 4.3g; Cholesterol 142mg; Calcium 89mg; Fibre 0.8g; Sodium 91mg.

Fresh Fig Filo Tart

Figs cook wonderfully well and taste superb in this tart – the riper the figs, the better.

Serves 6–8

five 35 x 25cm/14 x 10in sheets filo pastry, thawed if frozen
25g/1oz/2 tbsp butter, melted, plus extra for greasing
6 fresh figs, cut into wedges
75g/3oz/⅔ cup plain (all-purpose) flour
75g/3oz/6 tbsp caster (superfine) sugar
4 eggs
450ml/¾ pint/scant 2 cups milk
2.5ml/½ tsp almond extract
15ml/1 tbsp icing (confectioners') sugar, for dusting
whipped cream or Greek (US strained plain) yogurt, to serve

1 Preheat the oven to 190°C/375°F/Gas 5. Grease a 25 x 16cm/10 x 6¼in baking tin (pan) with butter. Brush each filo sheet in turn with melted butter and use to line the prepared tin.

2 Using scissors, cut off any excess pastry, leaving a little overhanging the edge. Arrange the figs in the filo case.

3 Sift the flour into a bowl and stir in the caster sugar. Add the eggs and a little of the milk and whisk until smooth. Gradually whisk in the remaining milk and the almond extract. Pour the mixture over the figs; bake for 1 hour or until the batter has set and is golden.

4 Remove the tart from the oven and allow it to cool in the tin on a wire rack for 10 minutes. Dust with the icing sugar and serve with whipped cream or Greek yogurt.

Cook's Tip
Filo pastry dries out quickly, so keep the sheets not currently being used covered under a clean damp dish towel. Also, work as quickly as possible. If the filo should turn dry and brittle, simply brush it with melted butter to moisten.

Filo-Topped Apple Pie

With its crisp, melt-in-the-mouth filo topping and minimal butter, this is a really light dessert, making it the perfect choice for those trying to combine a sweet tooth with a healthy eating plan. There's certainly no loss of flavour in this tasty variation on a traditional theme, so feel free to serve it to family and friends who will soon discover it tastes as good as it looks.

Serves 6

900g/2lb cooking apples
75g/3oz/6 tbsp caster (superfine) sugar
grated rind of 1 lemon
15ml/1 tbsp lemon juice
75g/3oz/½ cup sultanas (golden raisins)
2.5ml/½ tsp ground cinnamon
4 large sheets filo pastry, thawed if frozen
25g/1oz/2 tbsp butter, melted
icing (confectioners') sugar, for dusting

1 Peel, core and dice the apples. Place the apples in a pan with the caster sugar and lemon rind. Drizzle the lemon juice over.

2 Bring to the boil, stir well, then cook for 5 minutes, until the apples have softened.

3 Stir in the sultanas and cinnamon. Spoon the mixture into a 1.2 litre/2 pint/5 cup pie dish; level the top. Allow to cool.

4 Preheat the oven to 180°C/350°F/Gas 4. Place a pie funnel in the centre of the fruit. Brush each sheet of filo with melted butter.

5 Scrunch the filo up loosely and place on the fruit to cover it completely. Bake for 20–30 minutes until the filo is golden.

6 To serve, dust the pie with the icing sugar.

Cook's Tip
For a delightful change of flavour and texture, substitute flaked (sliced) almonds – plain or toasted – for some or all of the sultanas (golden raisins) in the pie.

Fig Tart Energy 213Kcal/900kJ; Protein 5.8g; Carbohydrate 36.7g, of which sugars 20g; Fat 5.9g, of which saturates 2.5g; Cholesterol 102mg; Calcium 89mg; Fibre 1.8g; Sodium 65mg.
Apple Pie Energy 210Kcal/892kJ; Protein 2.1g; Carbohydrate 44.8g, of which sugars 35.3g; Fat 3.8g, of which saturates 2.2g; Cholesterol 9mg; Calcium 39mg; Fibre 3g; Sodium 32mg.

One-Crust Rhubarb Pie

This method can be used for all sorts of fruit and is really foolproof. It doesn't matter how rough the pie looks when it goes into the oven; it always comes out looking fantastic!

Serves 6
350g/12oz shortcrust pastry, thawed if frozen
1 egg yolk, beaten
25g/1oz/3 tbsp semolina
25g/1oz/¼ cup hazelnuts, coarsely chopped
30ml/2 tbsp golden granulated sugar

For the filling
450g/1lb rhubarb, cut into 2.5cm/1in pieces
75g/3oz/6 tbsp caster (superfine) sugar
1–2 pieces preserved stem ginger in syrup, drained and finely chopped

1 Preheat the oven to 200°C/400°F/Gas 6. Roll out the pastry to a circle 35cm/14in across. Lay it over the rolling pin and transfer it to a large baking sheet. Brush a little egg yolk over the pastry. Scatter the semolina over the centre, leaving a wide rim all round the edge.

2 Make the filling. Place the rhubarb pieces, caster sugar and chopped ginger in a large bowl and mix well.

3 Pile the rhubarb mixture into the middle of the pastry. Fold the rim roughly over the filling so that it almost covers it. Some of the fruit will remain visible in the centre.

4 Brush the pastry rim with any remaining egg yolk to glaze, then scatter the hazelnuts and golden sugar over the top. Bake the pie for 30–35 minutes or until the pastry is golden brown. Serve hot or warm.

> **Cook's Tip**
> Egg yolk glaze brushed on to pastry gives it a nice golden sheen. However, be careful not to drip the glaze on the baking sheet, or it will burn and be difficult to remove.

Apricot Parcels

These little filo parcels contain a special apricot and mincemeat filling. A good way to use up any mincemeat and marzipan left over from Christmas!

Makes 8
350g/12oz filo pastry, thawed if frozen
50g/2oz/¼ cup butter, melted
8 apricots, halved and stoned (pitted)
60ml/4 tbsp luxury mincemeat
12 ratafia biscuits (almond macaroons), crushed
30ml/2 tbsp grated marzipan
icing (confectioners') sugar, for dusting

1 Preheat the oven to 200°C/400°F/Gas 6. Cut the filo pastry into 32 x 18cm/7in squares. Brush four of the squares with a little melted butter and stack them, giving each layer a quarter turn so that the stack acquires a star shape. Repeat this stacking process to make eight stars.

2 Place an apricot half, hollow up, in the centre of each pastry star. Mix together the mincemeat, crushed ratafias and marzipan and spoon a little of the mixture into the hollow of each apricot.

3 Top with another apricot half, then bring the corners of each pastry star together and squeeze to make a gathered purse.

4 Place the purses on a baking sheet and brush each with a little melted butter. Bake for 15–20 minutes or until the pastry is golden and crisp. Lightly dust with icing sugar to serve.

> **Cook's Tips**
> • Whipped cream, flavoured with a little brandy, makes an ideal accompaniment to the delicious parcels.
> • If ratafias are not available, use amaretti instead or simply leave them out, as the mincemeat adds lots of flavour.

Rhubarb Pie Energy 389Kcal/1633kJ; Protein 5.6g; Carbohydrate 49.7g, of which sugars 19.6g; Fat 20.1g, of which saturates 5.6g; Cholesterol 42mg; Calcium 139mg; Fibre 2.5g; Sodium 239mg.
Apricot Parcels Energy 214Kcal/902kJ; Protein 3.2g; Carbohydrate 34.9g, of which sugars 15.2g; Fat 7.9g, of which saturates 4.1g; Cholesterol 14mg; Calcium 56mg; Fibre 1.7g; Sodium 83mg.

Coconut Dumplings with Apricot Sauce

Based on a simple Asian recipe, these delicate little dumplings are very quick to cook. The sharp flavour of the sauce offsets the creamy dumplings beautifully.

Serves 4
75g/3oz/6 tbsp low-fat cottage cheese
I egg white
15ml/I tbsp low-fat spread
15ml/I tbsp light muscovado (brown) sugar

30ml/2 tbsp self-raising (self-rising) wholemeal (whole-wheat) flour
finely grated rind of ½ lemon
15ml/I tbsp desiccated (dry unsweetened shredded) coconut, toasted

For the sauce
225g/8oz can apricot halves in natural juice
15ml/I tbsp lemon juice

I Half-fill a steamer with boiling water and put it on to boil. If you do not own a steamer, place a heatproof plate over a pan of boiling water.

2 Beat together the cottage cheese, egg white and low-fat spread until they are evenly mixed.

3 Stir in the sugar, flour, lemon rind and coconut, mixing everything evenly to a fairly firm dough.

4 Place 8–12 spoonfuls of the mixture in the steamer or on the plate, leaving a space between them.

5 Cover the steamer or pan tightly with a lid or a plate and steam for about 10 minutes, until the dumplings have risen and are firm to the touch.

6 Make the sauce. Purée the can of apricots and stir in the lemon juice. Pour into a small pan and heat until boiling, then serve with the dumplings. Sprinkle with extra coconut to serve.

Apple & Walnut Crumble

An American favourite, combining delicious apples with crunchy walnuts for a simple, but tasty, dessert.

Serves 6
butter or margarine, for greasing
900g/2lb eating apples, peeled and sliced
grated rind of ½ lemon
15ml/I tbsp fresh lemon juice

115g/4oz/scant ½ cup soft light brown sugar
75g/3oz/⅔ cup plain (all-purpose) flour
1.5ml/¼ tsp salt
1.5ml/¼ tsp grated nutmeg
2.5ml/½ tsp ground cardamom
2.5ml/½ tsp ground cinnamon
30ml/2 tbsp butter or margarine
20g/¾oz/3 tbsp walnut pieces, chopped

I Preheat the oven to 180°C/350°F/Gas 4. Grease a 23cm/9in oval gratin dish or shallow baking dish. Toss the apples with the lemon rind and juice. Arrange the apples evenly in the bottom of the prepared dish.

2 Combine the brown sugar, flour, salt, nutmeg, cardamom and cinnamon in a mixing bowl. Rub in the butter or margarine with your fingertips until the mixture resembles coarse breadcrumbs. Stir in the chopped walnuts.

3 Using a large spoon, sprinkle the walnut and spice mixture evenly over the apples. Cover the dish with a piece of foil and bake for 30 minutes.

4 Remove the foil and continue baking for about 30 minutes more, until the apples are tender and the crumble topping is crisp. Serve warm.

Variations
To vary the crumble topping, replace the walnuts with rolled oats or use wholemeal (whole-wheat) flour instead of plain flour. For a citrus-flavoured crumble, replace the spices with finely grated lemon or orange rind. Try replacing some of the apples with blackberries, or add a handful of raisins to the filling.

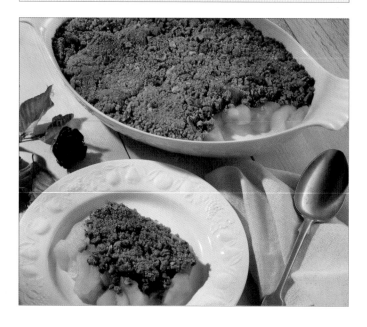

Coconut Dumplings Energy 134Kcal/565kJ; Protein 4.4g; Carbohydrate 19.5g, of which sugars 13.9g; Fat 4.7g, of which saturates 2.9g; Cholesterol 3mg; Calcium 66mg; Fibre 1.3g; Sodium 130mg.
Apple & Walnut Crumble Energy 231Kcal/977kJ; Protein 2.2g; Carbohydrate 43.3g, of which sugars 33.7g; Fat 6.7g, of which saturates 0.2g; Cholesterol 0mg; Calcium 37mg; Fibre 2.9g; Sodium 45mg.

Apple Strudel

Packed with spiced apples and nuts, this Austrian dessert is traditionally made with paper-thin layers of buttered strudel pastry, but featherlight filo pastry makes an easy substitute.

Serves 4–6
75g/3oz/¾ cup hazelnuts, chopped and roasted
30ml/2 tbsp nibbed almonds, roasted
50g/2oz/4 tbsp demerara (raw) sugar
2.5ml/½ tsp ground cinnamon
grated rind and juice of ½ lemon
2 large cooking apples, peeled, cored and chopped
50g/2oz/⅓ cup sultanas (golden raisins)
4 large sheets filo pastry
50g/2oz/4 tbsp unsalted (sweet) butter, melted
icing (confectioners') sugar, for dusting

1 Preheat the oven to 190°C/375°F/Gas 5. In a bowl mix together the hazelnuts, almonds, sugar, cinnamon, lemon rind and juice, apples and sultanas. Set aside.

2 Lay one sheet of filo pastry on a clean dish towel and brush with melted butter. Lay a second sheet on top and brush again with melted butter. Repeat with the remaining two sheets.

3 Spread the fruit and nut mixture over the pastry, leaving a 7.5cm/3in border at the shorter ends. Fold the ends in over the filling. Roll up from one long edge, using the dish towel.

4 Transfer the strudel to a greased baking sheet, placing it seam side down. Brush with butter and bake for 30–35 minutes, until golden and crisp. Dust with icing sugar and serve hot with cream, custard or yogurt.

Cook's Tip
Filo or strudel pastry is fiddly and time consuming to make, so it makes sense to use the ready-made version, which is very good and is now widely available. The filo dries out quickly, so keep the sheets covered with a damp dish towel as you work.

Spiced Apple Crumble

Any fruit can be used in this popular British dessert, but you can't beat the favourites of blackberry and apple. Hazelnuts and cardamom seeds give extra flavour.

Serves 4–6
450g/1lb cooking apples
115g/4oz/1 cup blackberries
grated rind and juice of 1 orange
50g/2oz/¼ cup light muscovado (brown) sugar

For the topping
175g/6oz/1½ cups plain (all-purpose) flour
75g/3oz/6 tbsp butter, plus extra for greasing
75g/3oz/6 tbsp caster (superfine) sugar
25g/1oz/¼ cup chopped hazelnuts
2.5ml/½ tsp crushed cardamom seeds
fresh custard, to serve

1 Preheat the oven to 200°C/400°F/Gas 6. Generously butter a 1.2 litre/2 pint/5 cup baking dish.

2 Peel and core the apples, then slice them into the prepared baking dish. Level the surface, then scatter the blackberries over. Sprinkle the orange rind and light muscovado sugar evenly over the top, then pour over the orange juice. Set aside.

3 Make the topping. Sift the flour into a bowl and rub in the butter until the mixture resembles coarse breadcrumbs. Stir in the caster sugar, hazelnuts and cardamom seeds. Scatter the topping over the top of the fruit.

4 Press the topping around the edges of the dish to seal in the juices. Bake for 30–35 minutes or until the crumble is golden. Serve hot, with custard.

Variations
This wonderfully good-natured pudding can be made with all sorts of fruit. Try plums, apricots, peaches or pears, alone or in combination with apples. Rhubarb makes a delectable crumble, especially when partnered with bananas.

Apple Crumble Energy 333Kcal/1401kJ; Protein 3.9g; Carbohydrate 52.4g, of which sugars 30.1g; Fat 13.4g, of which saturates 6.8g; Cholesterol 27mg; Calcium 71mg; Fibre 3g; Sodium 80mg.
Apple Strudel Energy 287Kcal/1199kJ; Protein 4.4g; Carbohydrate 29.1g, of which sugars 19.2g; Fat 17.8g, of which saturates 5.2g; Cholesterol 18mg; Calcium 60mg; Fibre 2.4g; Sodium 55mg.

Frozen Clementines

These pretty, sorbet-filled fruits store well in the freezer, so they make an ideal dessert to prepare in advance for a dinner party. Try to use organic citrus fruit, which will not be coated with anti-fungal wax.

Makes 12

*16 large clementines or
    small oranges
175g/6oz/³⁄₄ cup caster
    (superfine) sugar
105ml/7 tbsp water
juice of 2 lemons
a little fresh orange juice, if
    necessary
fresh mint leaves, to decorate*

1 Carefully slice the tops off 12 of the clementines to make lids. Place the lids on a baking sheet. Loosen the fruit flesh with a sharp knife then carefully scoop it out into a bowl, keeping the shells intact. Scrape out the membrane from the shells, then add the shells to the baking sheet and place in the freezer.

2 Put the sugar and water in a heavy pan and heat gently, stirring until the sugar dissolves. Boil for 3 minutes without stirring, then cool. Stir in the lemon juice.

3 Grate the rind from the remaining four clementines. Squeeze the fruits and add the juice and rind to the lemon syrup.

4 Process the clementine flesh in a food processor, then press it through a sieve (strainer) to extract the juice. Add this to the syrup. You need about 900ml/1 ½ pints/3³⁄₄ cups of liquid. Make up to the required amount with orange juice if necessary.

5 Pour the mixture into a freezer container and freeze for 3–4 hours, beating twice as the sorbet thickens. Alternatively, use an ice cream maker and churn the mixture until it holds its shape.

6 Spoon the citrus sorbet into the fruit shells, position the lids on top and return to the freezer for several hours, until solid.

7 Transfer to the refrigerator about 30 minutes before serving, to soften slightly. Decorate with fresh mint leaves to serve.

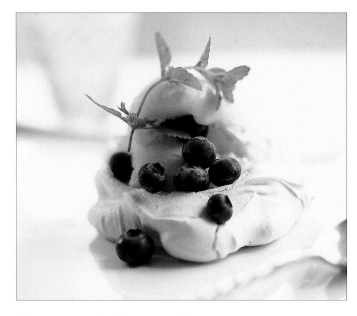

Orange & Yogurt Ice

With this low-fat ice, you can indulge in a dessert without feeling too guilty.

Serves 6
*90ml/6 tbsp water
10ml/2 tsp powdered gelatine
115g/4oz/generous ½ cup caster
    (superfine) sugar
250ml/8fl oz/1 cup freshly
    squeezed orange juice from
    a carton or bottle
500ml/17fl oz/generous 2 cups
    low-fat natural (plain) yogurt
cones or meringue nests,
    blueberries and fresh mint
    sprigs, to serve*

1 Put 30ml/2 tbsp of the water in a small bowl and sprinkle the powdered gelatine over the top. Set aside until spongy. Meanwhile, put the sugar in a small pan, add the remaining water and heat through gently until the sugar has dissolved.

2 Remove the pan from the heat, add the gelatine and stir until completely dissolved. Cool, stir in the orange juice and chill for 15–30 minutes.

3 Spoon the yogurt into a bowl, gradually add the chilled orange juice mixture and mix well. Pour the mixture into a freezer container. Freeze for 6 hours or until firm, beating twice with a fork or in a food processor to break up the ice crystals.

4 Alternatively, use an ice cream maker. Freeze the mixture until starting to thicken. Switch off the machine, remove the paddle, if necessary, add the yogurt and mix well. Replace the paddle and continue to churn the ice cream for 15–20 minutes until thick. Scrape it into a freezer container and freeze until firm.

5 Scoop the yogurt ice into cones or meringue nests and decorate with blueberries and mint.

> **Cook's Tip**
> *Meringue nests are not difficult to make, but if you do not have the time, bought ones are a perfectly acceptable alternative.*

Frozen Clementines Energy 117Kcal/499kJ; Protein 1.8g; Carbohydrate 28.9g, of which sugars 28.9g; Fat 0.2g, of which saturates 0g; Cholesterol 0mg; Calcium 83mg; Fibre 2.7g; Sodium 9mg.
Orange & Yogurt Ice Energy 137Kcal/583kJ; Protein 4.6g; Carbohydrate 30g, of which sugars 30g; Fat 0.9g, of which saturates 0.4g; Cholesterol 1mg; Calcium 173mg; Fibre 0.1g; Sodium 75mg.

Watermelon Sorbet

This pretty pink sorbet makes a fresh-tasting dessert, but it could also be served before the main course at a smart dinner party, to cleanse the palate.

Serves 6

1kg/2¼lb piece watermelon
200g/7oz/1 cup caster (superfine) sugar
120ml/4fl oz/½ cup water
juice of 1 lemon
2 egg whites
mint leaves, to decorate

1 Using a sharp knife, cut the watermelon into wedges, then cut the flesh away from the rind. Cube the flesh, picking out all the seeds at the same time.

2 Purée three-quarters of the flesh in a food processor or blender, but mash the last quarter on a plate – this will give the sorbet more texture.

3 Stir the sugar with the lemon juice and water in a pan over very low heat until the sugar dissolves and the syrup is clear.

4 Mix all the watermelon and the syrup in a large bowl and transfer to a freezer container.

5 Freeze for 1–1½ hours, until the edges begin to set. Beat the mixture, return to the freezer and freeze for a further 1 hour.

6 Whisk the egg whites to soft peaks. Beat the iced mixture again and fold in the egg whites. Return to the freezer for a further hour, then beat once more and freeze until firm.

7 Transfer the sorbet to the refrigerator about 20–30 minutes before serving. Serve in scoops decorated with mint leaves.

> **Cook's Tip**
> *Work quickly when beating the frozen mixture – you do not want it to completely melt before you return it to the freezer.*

Blackcurrant Sorbet

Blackcurrants produce a vibrant and intensely flavoured sorbet that is ideal for rounding off an *alfresco* summer meal.

Serves 4–6

90g/3½oz/½ cup caster (superfine) sugar
120ml/4fl oz/½ cup water
500g/1¼lb blackcurrants
juice of ½ lemon
15ml/1 tbsp egg white
mint leaves, to decorate

1 Place the sugar and water in a pan over medium-high heat and bring to the boil, stirring until the sugar has dissolved. Continue to boil the syrup for 2 minutes, then remove the pan from the heat and set aside to cool.

2 Remove the blackcurrants from their stalks, by pulling them through the tines of a fork.

3 Put the blackcurrants and lemon juice in a blender or food processor fitted with a metal blade, and process until smooth. Alternatively, chop the blackcurrants coarsely, then add the lemon juice. Mix in the sugar syrup.

4 Press through a sieve (strainer) to remove the seeds.

5 Pour the blackcurrant purée into a non-metallic freezer container. Cover with clear film (plastic wrap) or a lid and freeze until the sorbet is nearly firm, but still a bit slushy.

6 Cut the sorbet into pieces and put in the blender or food processor. Process until smooth, then, with the machine running, add the egg white and process until well mixed. Transfer the sorbet back to the freezer container and freeze until almost firm. Chop the sorbet again and process until smooth. Return to the freezer again until firm.

7 Serve immediately or freeze, tightly covered, for up to one week. Allow to soften for 5–10 minutes at room temperature before serving, decorated with mint leaves.

Watermelon Sorbet Energy 187Kcal/798kJ; Protein 2g; Carbohydrate 46.7g, of which sugars 46.7g; Fat 0.5g, of which saturates 0.2g; Cholesterol 0mg; Calcium 30mg; Fibre 0.2g; Sodium 26mg.
Blackcurrant Sorbet Energy 84Kcal/361kJ; Protein 1.3g; Carbohydrate 21.2g, of which sugars 21.2g; Fat 0g, of which saturates 0g; Cholesterol 0mg; Calcium 58mg; Fibre 3g; Sodium 14mg.

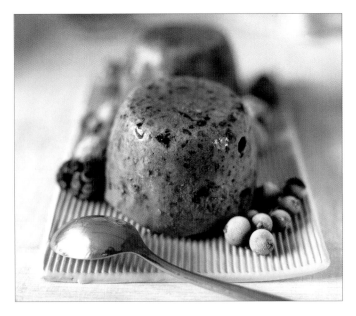

Summer Berry Frozen Yogurt

Any frozen summer fruits will work well for this dish.

Serves 6
350g/12oz/3 cups frozen
  summer fruits

200ml/7fl oz/scant 1 cup Greek
  (US strained plain) yogurt
25g/1oz icing (confectioners')
  sugar

1 Put all the ingredients into a food processor and process until combined but still quite chunky. Spoon the mixture into six 150ml/¼ pint/⅔ cup ramekin dishes. Cover each dish with clear film (plastic wrap) and place in the freezer for about 2 hours, or until firm.

2 To turn out the frozen yogurts, dip the dishes briefly in hot water and invert them on to small serving plates. Tap the base of the dishes and the yogurts will come out easily. Serve immediately.

Watermelon Ice

This refreshing dessert is perfect after a spicy meal.

Serves 4–6
105ml/7 tbsp water

90ml/6 tbsp caster (superfine)
  sugar
4 kaffir lime leaves, torn into small
  pieces
500g/1¼lb watermelon

1 Put the water, sugar and lime leaves in a pan. Heat gently until the sugar dissolves, then pour into a bowl and set aside to cool.

2 Cut the watermelon into wedges. Cut the flesh from the rind, remove the seeds and chop the flesh. Process the flesh to a slush in a food processor. Mix in the sugar syrup. Chill for 3–4 hours.

3 Strain into a freezer container and freeze for 2 hours, then beat with a fork to break up the ice crystals. Return to the freezer for 3 hours more, beating every 30 minutes, then freeze until firm. Place in the refrigerator 30 minutes before serving.

Elderflower & Lime Yogurt Ice

Fragrant elderflowers have a wonderful flavour, but they are in season for only a very short time. Fortunately, good-quality ready-made elderflower cordial is readily available and combines beautifully with limes to make a lovely iced dessert.

Serves 6
4 egg yolks
50g/2oz/¼ cup caster
  (superfine) sugar

10ml/2 tsp cornflour (cornstarch)
300ml/½ pint/1¼ cups milk
finely grated rind and juice of
  2 limes
150ml/¼ pint/⅔ cup elderflower
  cordial
200ml/7fl oz/scant 1 cup Greek
  (US strained plain) yogurt
150ml/¼ pint/⅔ cup double
  (heavy) cream
grated lime rind, to decorate

1 Whisk the egg yolks in a bowl with the sugar, cornflour and a little of the milk. Pour the remaining milk into a heavy pan, bring it to the boil, then pour it over the yolk mixture, whisking constantly. Return the mixture to the pan and cook over a very gentle heat, stirring constantly until the custard thickens. Do not let it boil or it may curdle.

2 Pour the custard into a bowl and add the lime rind and juice. Pour in the elderflower cordial and mix lightly. Cover the surface of the mixture closely with baking parchment. Leave to cool, then chill until very cold.

3 Whip together the yogurt and cream and fold into the custard. Pour the mixture into a freezer container and freeze for 3–4 hours, beating twice as it thickens. Scoop into individual dishes and return to the freezer until ready to serve.

4 Alternatively, use an ice cream maker. Stir the yogurt and cream into the custard and churn until it thickens. Transfer the yogurt ice into individual dishes and freeze until required.

5 Transfer the yogurt ice to the refrigerator 30 minutes before serving. Decorate with the grated lime rind and serve.

Summer Berry Yogurt Energy 71Kcal/295kJ; Protein 2.6g; Carbohydrate 8.5g, of which sugars 8.5g; Fat 3.5g, of which saturates 1.7g; Cholesterol 0mg; Calcium 62mg; Fibre 0.7g; Sodium 28mg.
Watermelon Ice Energy 85Kcal/363kJ; Protein 0.5g; Carbohydrate 21.6g, of which sugars 21.6g; Fat 0.3g, of which saturates 0.1g; Cholesterol 0mg; Calcium 14mg; Fibre 0.1g; Sodium 3mg.
Elderflower & Lime Ice Energy 219Kcal/912kJ; Protein 4.3g; Carbohydrate 12.4g, of which sugars 10.9g; Fat 17.7g, of which saturates 10.6g; Cholesterol 37mg; Calcium 125mg; Fibre 0g; Sodium 54mg.

Tangerine Trifle

An unusual variation on a traditional trifle – of course, you can add a little alcohol if you wish.

Serves 4
5 trifle sponges, halved lengthways
30ml/2 tbsp apricot jam
15–20 ratafia biscuits (almond macaroons)

142g/4¾oz packet tangerine jelly (flavoured gelatine)
300g/11oz can mandarin oranges, drained, reserving juice
600ml/1 pint/2½ cups fresh ready-made custard
whipped cream and shreds of orange rind, to decorate
caster (superfine) sugar, for sprinkling

1 Spread the halved sponge cakes with apricot jam and arrange in the base of a deep serving bowl or glass dish. Sprinkle over the ratafia biscuits.

2 Break up the jelly into a heatproof measuring jug (cup). Add the juice from the canned mandarins and place in a pan of hot water or in the microwave to dissolve. Stir until clear.

3 Make up to 600ml/1 pint/2½ cups with ice cold water, stir well and leave to cool for up to 30 minutes. Scatter the mandarin oranges over the cakes and ratafias.

4 Pour the jelly over the mandarin oranges, cake and ratafias and chill for 1 hour.

5 When the jelly has set, pour the custard smoothly over the top and chill again.

6 When ready to serve, pipe the whipped cream over the custard. Wash the orange rind shreds, sprinkle them with caster sugar and use to decorate the trifle.

Cook's Tip
For an even better flavour, use your own homemade custard.

Lemon Soufflé with Blackberries

The simple fresh taste of cold lemon soufflé combines well with rich blackberry sauce, and the colour contrast looks wonderful, too. Blueberries or raspberries make equally delicious alternatives to blackberries.

Serves 6
grated rind of 1 lemon and juice of 2 lemons
15ml/1 tbsp/1 sachet powdered gelatine

5 eggs, separated
150g/5oz/¾ cup caster (superfine) sugar
few drops vanilla extract
400ml/14fl oz/1⅔ cups whipping cream

For the sauce
175g/6oz/¾ cup blackberries (fresh or frozen)
30–45ml/2–3 tbsp caster (superfine) sugar
few fresh blackberries and blackberry leaves, to decorate

1 Place the lemon juice in a small pan and heat through. Sprinkle on the gelatine and leave to dissolve or heat further until clear. Allow to cool.

2 Put the lemon rind, egg yolks, sugar and vanilla into a large bowl and whisk until the mixture is very thick, pale and creamy.

3 Whisk the egg whites until stiff and almost peaky. Whip the cream until stiff.

4 Stir the gelatine mixture into the yolks, then fold in the whipped cream and lastly the egg whites. Turn into a 1.5 litre/ 2½ pint/6¼ cup soufflé dish and freeze for about 2 hours.

5 To make the sauce, place the blackberries in a pan with the sugar and cook for 4–6 minutes, until the juices begin to run and all the sugar has dissolved. Pass through a sieve (strainer) to remove the seeds, then chill.

6 When the soufflé is almost frozen, but still spoonable, scoop or spoon out on to individual plates and serve with the blackberry sauce, decorated with fresh blackberries and blackberry leaves.

Tangerine Trifle Energy 579Kcal/2451kJ; Protein 14.1g; Carbohydrate 111g, of which sugars 81.1g; Fat 10.3g, of which saturates 2.7g; Cholesterol 145mg; Calcium 241mg; Fibre 1.3g; Sodium 211mg.
Lemon Soufflé Energy 381Kcal/1592kJ; Protein 7.4g; Carbohydrate 35g, of which sugars 35g; Fat 24.6g, of which saturates 18.9g; Cholesterol 164mg; Calcium 104mg; Fibre 1g; Sodium 98mg.

Rhubarb & Orange Fool

This traditional English dessert is extremely easy to make, yet is utterly mouthwatering with its distinctive taste and texture.

Serves 4
30ml/2 tbsp freshly squeezed orange juice
5ml/1 tsp finely shredded orange rind

1kg/2¼lb (about 10–12 stems) rhubarb, chopped
15ml/1 tbsp redcurrant jelly
45ml/3 tbsp caster (superfine) sugar
150g/5oz/⅔ cup ready-to-serve thick and creamy custard
150ml/¼ pint/⅔ cup double (heavy) cream, whipped
crisp biscuits (cookies), to serve

1 Place the orange juice and rind, the rhubarb, redcurrant jelly and sugar in a pan. Cover and simmer gently for about 8 minutes, stirring occasionally, until the rhubarb is just tender but not mushy.

2 Remove the pan from the heat, transfer the rhubarb to a bowl and leave to cool completely.

3 Drain the cooled rhubarb to remove some of the liquid. Reserve a few pieces of the rhubarb and a little orange rind for decoration. Purée the remaining rhubarb in a food processor or blender, or push through a sieve (strainer).

4 Stir the custard into the purée, then fold in the whipped cream. Spoon the fool into individual bowls, cover and chill. Just before serving, top with the reserved fruit and rind. Serve with crisp, sweet biscuits.

> **Variation**
> This dessert also works well with gooseberries – another classic English fruit – instead of the rhubarb. Cook the gooseberries with about 60ml/4 tbsp water instead of the orange juice and increase the sugar to taste. Leave out the grated orange rind as well, and decorate with chopped nuts.

Apricots with Orange Cream

Creamy mascarpone cheese, delicately flavoured with orange juice, makes a delicious topping for chilled apricots. Here, the apricots themselves are infused with the subtle flavours of orange and cinnamon, with dessert wine added for a taste of sweet luxury.

Serves 4
450g/1lb/2 cups ready-to-eat dried apricots

strip of orange peel
1 cinnamon stick
45ml/3 tbsp caster (superfine) sugar
450ml/¾ pint/scant 2 cups water
150ml/¼ pint/⅔ cup sweet dessert wine
115g/4oz/½ cup mascarpone cheese
45ml/3 tbsp orange juice
pinch of ground cinnamon and fresh mint sprig, to decorate

1 Place the apricots, orange peel, cinnamon stick and 15ml/1 tbsp of the sugar in a pan and cover with the water. Bring to the boil, cover and simmer gently for 25 minutes, or until the fruit is tender.

2 Remove from the heat and stir in the dessert wine. Leave until cold, then chill for at least 3–4 hours or overnight.

3 Mix together the mascarpone cheese, orange juice and the remaining sugar in a bowl and beat thoroughly until the mixture is smooth, then chill.

4 Just before serving the dessert, remove the cinnamon stick and orange peel.

5 Serve with a spoonful of the orange cream sprinkled with cinnamon and decorated with a sprig of fresh mint.

> **Cook's Tip**
> The sweet wine Muscat de Beaumes de Venise is a good choice for this recipe, but any sweet muscat wine would do.

Rhubarb & Orange Energy 483Kcal/2008kJ; Protein 4.6g; Carbohydrate 24.4g, of which sugars 23.1g; Fat 41.2g, of which saturates 25.1g; Cholesterol 104mg; Calcium 311mg; Fibre 3.6g; Sodium 42mg.
Apricots with Or. Cream Energy 313Kcal/1326kJ; Protein 7.3g; Carbohydrate 56.9g, of which sugars 56.9g; Fat 4.9g, of which saturates 2.6g; Cholesterol 12mg; Calcium 95mg; Fibre 7.1g; Sodium 23mg.

Gooseberry & Orange Flower Cream

Fresh-tasting gooseberries and fragrant orange flower water give this dessert an attractive flavour. For the most effective presentation, serve the cream in individual dishes, prettily decorated with mint sprigs.

Serves 4
500g/1 1/4lb gooseberries, trimmed
300ml/1/2 pint/1 1/4 cups double (heavy) cream
about 115g/4oz/1 cup icing (confectioners') sugar, to taste
30ml/2 tbsp orange flower water
fresh mint sprigs, to decorate
almond biscuits (cookies), to serve

1 Place the gooseberries in a heavy pan, cover and cook over a low heat, shaking the pan occasionally, until the gooseberries are tender. Tip the gooseberries into a bowl, crush them, then leave to cool completely.

2 Beat the cream until soft peaks form, then fold in half the gooseberries. Sweeten the mixture with icing sugar to taste, and add the orange flower water. Sweeten the remaining gooseberries to taste.

3 Layer the cream mixture and the crushed gooseberries in four dessert dishes or tall glasses, and then cover and chill. Decorate with mint sprigs and serve accompanied by almond biscuits.

> **Cook's Tip**
> *If you prefer, the cooked gooseberries can be thoroughly puréed and then strained. This will give the cream a much smoother texture.*

> **Variation**
> *The orange flower water can be replaced by elderflower cordial and homemade custard used instead of the cream.*

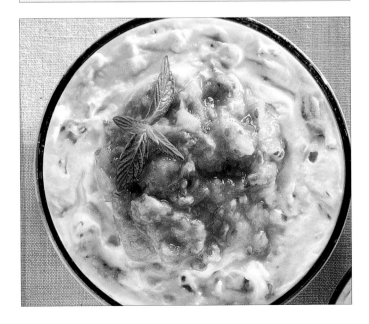

Fruity Ricotta Creams

Ricotta is an Italian soft cheese with a smooth texture and a mild, slightly sweet flavour. Served here with candied fruit peel and delicious chocolate, it is quite irresistible.

Serves 4
350g/12oz/1 1/2 cups ricotta cheese
30–45ml/2–3 tbsp Cointreau or other orange liqueur
10ml/2 tsp grated lemon rind
30ml/2 tbsp icing (confectioners') sugar
150ml/1/4 pint/2/3 cup double (heavy) cream
150g/5oz/scant 1 cup candied peel, such as orange, lemon and grapefruit, finely chopped
50g/2oz plain (semisweet) chocolate, finely chopped
chocolate curls, to decorate
amaretti, to serve (optional)

1 Using the back of a wooden spoon, push the ricotta through a fine sieve (strainer) into a large bowl.

2 Add the liqueur, lemon rind and icing sugar to the ricotta and beat well until the mixture is light and smooth.

3 Whip the cream in a large bowl until it forms soft peaks.

4 Gently fold the cream into the ricotta mixture with the candied peel and chopped chocolate.

5 Spoon the mixture into four individual glass dishes and chill for about 1 hour. Decorate the ricotta creams with chocolate curls and serve with amaretti, if you like.

> **Cook's Tips**
> *• For this uncooked, Italian-style dessert, you need to buy candied fruits in large pieces from a good delicatessen – tubs of chopped candied peel are too tough to eat raw, and should only be used in baking.*
> *• The desserts can also be topped with a sprinkling of raspberries to add an extra fruitiness.*

Gooseberry Cream Energy 518Kcal/2151kJ; Protein 2.7g; Carbohydrate 37.3g, of which sugars 37.3g; Fat 40.8g, of which saturates 25.1g; Cholesterol 103mg; Calcium 88mg; Fibre 3g; Sodium 21mg.
Ricotta Creams Energy 546Kcal/2276kJ; Protein 9.4g; Carbohydrate 43.1g, of which sugars 43g; Fat 36.7g, of which saturates 22.6g; Cholesterol 89mg; Calcium 75mg; Fibre 2.1g; Sodium 115mg.

Fig, Port & Clementine Sundaes

The distinctive flavours of figs, cinnamon, clementines and port are combined to make a refreshing sundae bursting with taste.

Serves six
6 clementines
30ml/2 tbsp clear honey
1 cinnamon stick, halved
15ml/1 tbsp light muscovado (brown) sugar
60ml/4 tbsp port
6 fresh figs
about 500ml/17fl oz/2¼ cups orange sorbet

1 Finely grate the rind from two clementines and put it in a small, heavy pan. Using a small, sharp knife, cut the peel away from all the clementines, then slice the flesh thinly.

2 Add the honey, cinnamon, sugar and port to the clementine rind. Heat gently until the sugar has completely dissolved, in order to make a syrup.

3 Put the clementine slices in a heatproof bowl and pour over the syrup. Cool completely, then chill.

4 Slice the figs thinly and add to the clementines and syrup, tossing the ingredients together gently. Leave for 10 minutes, then discard the cinnamon stick.

5 Arrange half the fig and clementine slices around the sides of six serving glasses. Half fill the glasses with scoops of sorbet. Arrange the remaining fruit slices around the sides of the glasses, then pile more sorbet into the centre. Pour over the port syrup and serve.

Cook's Tip
This rich and yet refreshing combination of ingredients creates the ideal dessert for finishing off a hearty winter meal on a light and fruity note.

Banana & Apricot Caramel Trifle

Bananas are transformed into a marvellous trifle.

Serves 6–8
300ml/½ pint/1¼ cups milk
1 vanilla pod (bean), or 4–5 drops vanilla extract
40g/1½oz/3 tbsp caster (superfine) sugar
20ml/4 tsp cornflour (cornstarch)
3 egg yolks
60ml/4 tbsp apricot jam
120ml/8 tbsp water
175–225g/6–8oz ginger cake, cubed
3 bananas, sliced, with one reserved for topping
115g/4oz/generous ½ cup granulated sugar
300ml/½ pint/1¼ cups double (heavy) cream
a few drops of lemon juice

1 Pour the milk into a small pan. Carefully split the vanilla pod (if using) down the middle and scrape the seeds into the pan.

2 Add the vanilla pod or extract to the milk and bring just to the boil, then remove the pan from the heat and set aside. When the milk has cooled slightly, remove the vanilla pod.

3 Whisk together the sugar, cornflour and egg yolks until pale and creamy. Whisk in the milk and return the mixture to the pan. Heat to simmering point, stirring constantly, and cook over a low heat until the custard coats the back of a wooden spoon thickly. Leave to cool, covering the surface with clear film (plastic wrap) to prevent a skin forming.

4 Put the apricot jam and 60ml/4 tbsp of the water in a pan and heat gently for 2–3 minutes, stirring. Put the cake in a deep serving bowl and pour on the apricot mixture. Cover with sliced bananas, then the custard. Chill for 1–2 hours.

5 Melt the sugar in a small pan with the remaining water and cook until just turning golden. Immediately pour on to a sheet of foil. Leave to harden, then break the caramel into pieces.

6 Whip the cream, then spread over the custard. Chill the trifle for 2–3 hours, then top with the remaining sliced banana, dipped into lemon juice, and the cracked caramel pieces.

Cherry Syllabub

This recipe follows the style of the earliest syllabubs from the sixteenth and seventeenth centuries, producing a frothy, creamy layer over a liquid one. Ripe cherries sprinkled with fiery Kirsch form the delicious bottom layer.

Serves 4
225g/8oz ripe dark cherries, pitted and chopped
30ml/2 tbsp Kirsch
2 egg whites
75g/3oz/6 tbsp caster (superfine) sugar
30ml/2 tbsp fresh lemon juice
150ml/¼ pint/⅔ cup sweet white wine
300ml/½ pint/1¼ cups double (heavy) cream

1 Divide the chopped cherries among six tall dessert glasses and sprinkle over the Kirsch.

2 In a clean, grease-free bowl, whisk the egg whites until stiff. Gently fold in the sugar, lemon juice and wine.

3 In a separate bowl (but using the same whisk), lightly beat the cream then fold into the egg white mixture.

4 Spoon the cream mixture over the cherries, then chill overnight. Serve straight from the refrigerator.

Cook's Tip
Be careful not to over-beat the egg whites otherwise they will separate, which will spoil the consistency of the dessert. Whip the cream until it is just forming soft peaks.

Variation
You can use crushed fresh raspberries or chopped ripe peaches or strawberries instead of the cherries. Ratafia biscuits (almond macaroons) make the perfect accompaniment.

Apricot & Orange Jelly

A light and refreshing dessert for a summer's day.

Serves 4
350g/12oz well-flavoured fresh ripe apricots, stoned (pitted)
50–75g/2–3oz/about ⅓ cup granulated sugar
about 300ml/½ pint/1¼ cups freshly squeezed orange juice
15ml/1 tbsp/1 sachet powdered gelatine
single (light) cream, to serve
finely chopped candied orange peel, to decorate

1 Put the apricots in a pan with the sugar and 120ml/4fl oz/½ cup of the orange juice. Place over medium heat and stir until the sugar has dissolved. Simmer very gently until the apricots are tender.

2 Press the apricot mixture through a nylon sieve (strainer) into a small measuring jug (cup) using a spoon.

3 Pour 45ml/3 tbsp of the orange juice into a small heatproof bowl, sprinkle over the gelatine and leave for about 5 minutes, until softened.

4 Place the bowl over a pan of hot water and heat until the gelatine has dissolved. Slowly pour into the apricot mixture, stirring constantly. Make up to 600ml/1 pint/2½ cups with the remaining orange juice.

5 Pour the apricot mixture into four individual dishes and chill until set.

6 To serve, pour a thin layer of cream over the surface, and decorate with candied orange peel.

Cook's Tip
Make sure that the gelatine is completely dissolved in the orange juice – there should be no sign of any granules and the liquid should be completely clear. The mixture must not boil.

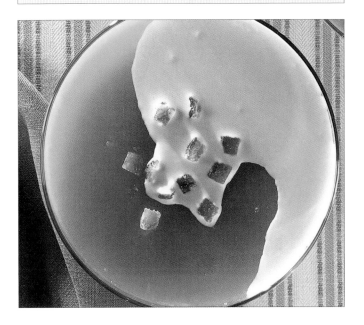

Cherry Syllabub Energy 514Kcal/2132kJ; Protein 3.3g; Carbohydrate 29.6g, of which sugars 29.6g; Fat 40.3g, of which saturates 25.1g; Cholesterol 103mg; Calcium 60mg; Fibre 0.5g; Sodium 54mg.
Apricot & Orange Jelly Energy 104Kcal/442kJ; Protein 1.2g; Carbohydrate 26g, of which sugars 26g; Fat 0.2g, of which saturates 0g; Cholesterol 0mg; Calcium 27mg; Fibre 1.6g; Sodium 10mg.

Banana & Mascarpone Creams

If you are a fan of cold banana custard, then you'll love this recipe. It is a grown-up version of an old favourite. No one will guess that the secret is simply ready-made custard.

Serves 4–6

250g/9oz/generous 1 cup mascarpone
300ml/½ pint/1¼ cups fresh ready-made custard
150ml/¼ pint/⅔ cup Greek (US strained plain) yogurt
4 bananas
juice of 1 lime
50g/2oz/½ cup pecan nuts, coarsely chopped
120ml/4fl oz/½ cup maple syrup

1 Combine the mascarpone, custard and yogurt in a large bowl and beat together until smooth. Make this mixture up to several hours ahead, if you like. Cover and chill, then stir well before using.

2 Slice the bananas diagonally and place in a separate bowl. Pour over the lime juice and toss together until the bananas are coated in the juice.

3 Divide half the custard mixture among four or six dessert glasses and top each portion with a generous spoonful of the banana and lime mixture.

4 Spoon the remaining custard mixture into the glasses and top with the rest of the bananas. Sprinkle the nuts over the top. Drizzle maple syrup over each dessert and chill for 30 minutes before serving.

Variations
Use clear honey instead of maple syrup and walnuts instead of pecan nuts, if you like. Also, try layering in some crumbled biscuits, such as amaretti or ratafia biscuits (almond macaroons), shortbread crumbs or crushed meringues.

Lemon Coeur à la Crème with Cointreau Oranges

This zesty dessert is the ideal choice to follow all kinds of main courses, but in particular a rich dish such as a meat roast.

Serves 4
225g/8oz/1 cup cottage cheese
250g/9oz/generous 1 cup mascarpone
50g/2oz/¼ cup caster (superfine) sugar
grated rind and juice of 1 lemon
spirals of orange rind, to decorate

For the Cointreau oranges
4 oranges
10ml/2 tsp cornflour (cornstarch)
15ml/1 tbsp icing (confectioners') sugar
60ml/4 tbsp Cointreau

1 Put the cottage cheese in a food processor or blender and process until smooth. Add the mascarpone, caster sugar, lemon rind and juice and process briefly to mix the ingredients.

2 Line four coeur à la crème moulds with muslin (cheesecloth), and divide the mixture among them. Level the surface of each, then place the moulds on a plate to catch any liquid that drains from the cheese. Cover and chill overnight.

3 Make the Cointreau oranges. Squeeze the juice from two oranges and pour into a measuring cup. Make the juice up to 250ml/8fl oz/1 cup with water, then pour into a small pan. Blend a little of the juice mixture with the cornflour and add to the pan with the icing sugar. Heat the sauce, stirring until thick.

4 Using a sharp knife, peel the remaining oranges. Cut between the membrane and fruit to separate the orange segments. Discard the membrane and white pith. Add the segments to the pan, stir to coat, then set aside. When cool, stir in the Cointreau. Cover and chill overnight.

5 Turn the moulds out on to plates and surround with the oranges. Serve decorated with spirals of orange rind.

Banana Creams Energy 457Kcal/1902kJ; Protein 12.4g; Carbohydrate 32.1g, of which sugars 30g; Fat 32.1g, of which saturates 9.1g; Cholesterol 19mg; Calcium 177mg; Fibre 1.2g; Sodium 142mg.
Lemon Coeur Energy 333Kcal/1400kJ; Protein 14.3g; Carbohydrate 36.8g, of which sugars 34.5g; Fat 11.4g, of which saturates 7g; Cholesterol 35mg; Calcium 137mg; Fibre 2.1g; Sodium 178mg.

Peach Melba Syllabub

If you are making these sophisticated temptations for a dinner party, cook the peaches and raspberries the day before to allow the fruit to chill. Whip up the syllabub at the very last minute to make a delicious, light-as-a-cloud topping.

Serves 6

4 peaches, peeled, stoned (pitted) and sliced
300ml/½ pint/1¼ cups blush or red grape juice
115g/4oz/⅔ cup raspberries
raspberry or mint leaves, to decorate
ratafia biscuits (almond macaroons) or other small crisp biscuits (cookies), to serve

For the syllabub
60ml/4 tbsp peach schnapps
30ml/2 tbsp blush or red grape juice
300ml/½ pint/1¼ cups double (heavy) cream

1 Place the peach slices in a large pan. Add the grape juice. Bring to the boil, then cover, lower the heat and simmer for 5–7 minutes or until tender.

2 Add the raspberries and remove from the heat. Set aside in the refrigerator until cold. Divide the peach and raspberry mixture among six dessert glasses.

3 For the syllabub, place the peach schnapps and grape juice in a large bowl and whisk in the cream until it forms soft peaks.

4 Spoon the syllabub on top of the fruit and decorate each portion with a fresh raspberry or mint leaf. Serve with ratafias or other crisp biscuits.

Variations
Use pears and sliced kiwi fruit in place of peaches and raspberries. Instead of the syllabub, try topping the fruit with whipped cream flavoured with Advocaat and finely chopped preserved stem ginger.

Fragrant Fruit Salad

A medley of colourful and exotic fruit, this fresh-tasting salad is the perfect dessert for a dinner party.

Serves 6

130g/4½oz/scant ¾ cup sugar
thinly pared rind and juice of 1 lime
150ml/¼ pint/⅔ cup water
60ml/4 tbsp brandy
5ml/1 tsp instant coffee granules or powder dissolved in 30ml/2 tbsp boiling water
1 small pineapple
1 papaya
2 pomegranates
1 medium mango
2 passion fruit or kiwi fruit
strips of lime rind, to decorate

1 Put the sugar and lime rind in a small pan with the water. Heat gently until the sugar dissolves, then bring to the boil and simmer for 5 minutes. Leave to cool, then strain into a large serving bowl, discarding the lime rind. Stir in the lime juice, brandy and dissolved coffee.

2 Using a sharp knife, cut the plume and stalk ends from the pineapple. Cut off the peel, then remove the central core and discard. Slice the flesh into bitesize pieces and add to the bowl.

3 Halve the papaya and scoop out the seeds. Cut away the skin, then slice the papaya. Halve the pomegranates and scoop out the seeds. Add to the bowl.

4 Cut the mango lengthways into three pieces, along each side of the stone (pit). Peel the skin off the flesh. Cut into chunks and add to the bowl.

5 Halve the passion fruit and scoop out the flesh using a teaspoon, or peel and chop the kiwi fruit. Add to the bowl and serve, decorated with lime rind.

Cook's Tip
Allow the salad to stand at room temperature for an hour before serving so the flavours can blend.

Peach Melba Energy 329Kcal/1363kJ; Protein 2g; Carbohydrate 17g, of which sugars 17g; Fat 27g, of which saturates 16.7g; Cholesterol 69mg; Calcium 45mg; Fibre 1.6g; Sodium 17mg.
Fragrant Fruit Salad Energy 218Kcal/930kJ; Protein 1.4g; Carbohydrate 49.8g, of which sugars 49.8g; Fat 0.4g, of which saturates 0g; Cholesterol 0mg; Calcium 60mg; Fibre 4.4g; Sodium 10mg.

Fruit Kebabs with Mango & Yogurt Sauce

These mixed fresh fruit kebabs make a versatile dessert that is as attractive as it is healthy.

Serves 4
1/2 pineapple, peeled, cored and cubed
2 kiwi fruit, peeled and cubed
175g/6oz/1 1/2 cups strawberries, hulled and cut in half, if large
1/2 mango, peeled, stoned (pitted) and cubed

For the sauce
120ml/4fl oz/1/2 cup fresh mango purée, from 1–1 1/2 peeled and stoned (pitted) mangoes
120ml/4fl oz/1/2 cup thick natural (plain) yogurt
5ml/1 tsp caster (superfine) sugar
few drops vanilla extract
15ml/1 tbsp finely chopped mint leaves

1 Make the sauce. Beat together the mango purée, yogurt, sugar and vanilla with an electric mixer.

2 Stir in the chopped mint. Cover the sauce and place in the refrigerator until required.

3 Thread the prepared fruit on to twelve 15cm/6in wooden skewers, alternating the pineapple, kiwi fruit, strawberries and mango cubes.

4 Arrange the kebabs on a large serving tray with the mango and yogurt sauce in the centre.

Variations
• Vary the type of fruit as you wish – melon, grapes and papaya would be suitable. The fruit must have a firm enough texture to stand up to being skewered.
• Try replacing the mango cubes with ripe peaches and serve with a pink sauce, by adding puréed and strained raspberries to the sauce instead of the mango purée. Leave out the mint.

Russian Fruit Compote

Traditionally called "Kissel" in Russia, this fruit dish is made from the thickened juice of stewed red- or blackcurrants. This version uses the whole fruit with an added dash of blackberry liqueur to give added zing.

Serves 4
225g/8oz/2 cups red- or blackcurrants or a mixture of both
225g/8oz/1 1/3 cups raspberries
50g/2oz/1/4 cup caster (superfine) sugar
150ml/1/4 pint/2/3 cup water
25ml/1 1/2 tbsp arrowroot
15–30ml/1–2 tbsp Crème de Mûre
Greek (US strained plain) yogurt, to serve

1 Place the red- or blackcurrants, raspberries and sugar in a pan with the water. Cover the pan and cook gently over a low heat for 12–15 minutes, until the fruit is soft.

2 Blend the arrowroot with a little water in a bowl and stir into the fruit off the heat. Bring the syrup back to the boil, stirring frequently until thickened.

3 Remove from the heat and cool slightly, then gently stir in the Crème de Mûre liqueur.

4 Pour into four serving bowls and leave until cold, then chill. Serve topped with spoonfuls of Greek yogurt.

Cook's Tips
• If you have difficulty finding Crème de Mûre, use the more well-known blackcurrant liqueur, Crème de Cassis, instead.
• Unlike cornflour (cornstarch), arrowroot thickens a liquid without making it cloudy, producing a clear glossy sauce.
• When preparing clusters of currants, remove the fruit from the stalks by running them through the prongs of a fork. There is no need to trim the fruit.

Fruit Kebabs Energy 120Kcal/513kJ; Protein 3g; Carbohydrate 27.1g, of which sugars 26.9g; Fat 0.8g, of which saturates 0.2g; Cholesterol 0mg; Calcium 97mg; Fibre 3.7g; Sodium 32mg.
Russian Fruit Compote Energy 91Kcal/389kJ; Protein 1.4g; Carbohydrate 20.3g, of which sugars 20.3g; Fat 0.2g, of which saturates 0.1g; Cholesterol 0mg; Calcium 55mg; Fibre 3.4g; Sodium 4mg.

Poached Pears in Port Syrup

The perfect choice for autumn entertaining, this simple dessert has a beautiful rich colour and fantastic flavour thanks to the tastes of port and lemon.

175ml/6fl oz/¾ cup ruby port
50g/2oz/¼ cup caster (superfine) sugar
1 cinnamon stick
60ml/4 tbsp cold water
cream, to serve

Serves 4
2 ripe, firm pears, such as Williams or Comice
pared rind of 1 lemon

To decorate
30ml/2 tbsp flaked (sliced) hazelnuts, toasted
fresh mint, pear or rose leaves

1 Peel the pears, cut them in half and remove the cores. Place the lemon rind, port, sugar, cinnamon stick and water in a shallow pan. Bring to the boil over a low heat. Add the pears, lower the heat, cover and poach for 5 minutes. Let the pears cool in the syrup.

2 When the pears are cold, transfer them to a bowl with a slotted spoon. Return the syrup to the heat. Boil rapidly until it has reduced to form a syrup that will coat the back of a spoon lightly. Remove the cinnamon stick and lemon rind and leave the syrup to cool.

3 To serve, place a pear half on a board, cut side down. Keeping it intact at the stalk end, slice the pear lengthways, then, using a palette knife, carefully transfer to a dessert plate. Press gently so that the pear fans out. Repeat with the remaining pears.

4 When all the pears have been fanned, spoon over the port syrup. Top each portion with a few hazelnuts and decorate with fresh mint, pear or rose leaves. Serve with cream.

> **Cook's Tip**
> *Choose pears of a similar size, with the stalks intact, for the most attractive effect when fanned on the plate.*

Papayas in Jasmine Flower Syrup

The fragrant syrup can be prepared in advance, using fresh jasmine flowers from a house plant or the garden. It tastes fabulous with papayas, but is also good with other tropical fruit, such as mangoes or lychees, or even ripe peaches.

Serves 2
105ml/7 tbsp water
45ml/3 tbsp palm sugar or light muscovado (brown) sugar
20–30 jasmine flowers, plus a few extra to decorate (optional)
2 ripe papayas
juice of 1 lime

1 Place the water and sugar in a small pan. Heat gently, stirring occasionally, until the sugar has dissolved, then simmer, without stirring, over a low heat for 4 minutes.

2 Pour into a bowl, leave to cool slightly, then add the jasmine flowers. Leave to steep for at least 20 minutes.

3 Peel the papayas and slice in half lengthways. Scoop out and discard the seeds. Place the papayas on serving plates and squeeze over the lime.

4 Strain the syrup into a clean bowl, discarding the flowers. Spoon the syrup over the papayas. Decorate with a few fresh jasmine flowers, if you like.

> **Cook's Tip**
> *Although scented white jasmine flowers are perfectly safe to eat, it is important to make sure that they have not been sprayed with pesticides or other harmful chemicals. Washing them may not remove all the residue.*

> **Variation**
> *Use the delicately flavoured syrup to turn simple ice cream into an exotic dessert – simply spoon over individual servings.*

Poached Pears Energy 158Kcal/666kJ; Protein 0.4g; Carbohydrate 28.3g, of which sugars 28.3g; Fat 0.1g, of which saturates 0g; Cholesterol 0mg; Calcium 20mg; Fibre 2.2g; Sodium 6mg.
Papayas in Syrup Energy 269Kcal/1143kJ; Protein 2.6g; Carbohydrate 67.5g, of which sugars 67.5g; Fat 0.5g, of which saturates 0g; Cholesterol 0mg; Calcium 127mg; Fibre 11g; Sodium 27mg.

Exotic Fruit Salad with Passion Fruit Dressing

Passion fruit makes a superb dressing for any fruit, but really brings out the flavour of exotic varieties. You can easily double the recipe and serve the rest for breakfast.

Serves 6
1 mango
1 papaya
2 kiwi fruit

coconut or vanilla ice cream,
 to serve

For the dressing
3 passion fruit
thinly pared rind and juice of
 1 lime
5ml/1 tsp hazelnut or walnut oil
15ml/1 tbsp clear honey

1 Peel the mango, cut it into three slices, then cut the flesh into chunks and place it in a large bowl. Peel the papaya and cut it in half. Scoop out the seeds, then chop the flesh.

2 Cut both ends off each kiwi fruit, then stand them on a board. Using a small sharp knife, cut off the skin from top to bottom. Cut each kiwi fruit in half lengthways, then cut into thick slices. Combine all the fruit in a large bowl.

3 Make the dressing. Cut each passion fruit in half and scoop the seeds out into a sieve (strainer) set over a small bowl. Press the seeds well to extract all their juices.

4 Lightly whisk the remaining dressing ingredients into the passion fruit juice, then pour the dressing over the fruit in the bowl. Mix gently to combine. Leave to chill for approximately 1 hour before serving with generous scoops of coconut or vanilla ice cream.

Cook's Tip
A clear golden honey scented with orange blossom or acacia blossom would be perfect for the dressing.

Ruby Fruit Salad

After a rich main course, this port-flavoured fruit salad is light and refreshing.

Serves 8
115g/4oz/generous 1/2 cup caster
 (superfine) sugar
1 cinnamon stick
4 cloves
pared rind of 1 orange

300ml/1/2 pint/1 1/4 cups water
300ml/1/2 pint/1 1/4 cups port
2 oranges
1 small ripe Ogen, Charentais
 or honeydew melon
4 small bananas
2 eating apples
225g/8oz seedless grapes

1 Put the sugar, spices, pared orange rind and the water into a pan and stir over a gentle heat to dissolve the sugar. Then bring to the boil, cover with a lid and simmer for 10 minutes. Leave to cool, then add the port.

2 Strain the liquid (to remove the spices and orange rind) into a bowl. With a sharp knife, cut off all the skin and pith from the oranges. Then, holding each orange over the bowl to catch the juice, cut away the segments by slicing between the membrane that divides each segment and allowing the segments to drop into the syrup. Squeeze the remaining pith to release any juice.

3 Cut the melon in half, remove the seeds and scoop out the flesh with a melon baller, or cut into small cubes. Add the melon to the syrup.

4 Peel the bananas and cut them diagonally in 1cm/1/2in slices. Quarter and core the apples, then peel if the skin is tough. Cut into small cubes. Halve the grapes if large or leave them whole. Stir all the fruit into the syrup, cover with clear film (plastic wrap) and chill for 1 hour before serving.

Cook's Tip
The port-flavoured syrup is very versatile and will marry well with any combination of fruit that is available.

Exotic Fruit Salad Energy 64Kcal/270kJ; Protein 1g; Carbohydrate 14.2g, of which sugars 14g; Fat 0.8g, of which saturates 0.1g; Cholesterol 0mg; Calcium 25mg; Fibre 2.8g; Sodium 7mg.
Ruby Fruit Salad Energy 209Kcal/886kJ; Protein 1.7g; Carbohydrate 42.1g, of which sugars 41g; Fat 0.3g, of which saturates 0.1g; Cholesterol 0mg; Calcium 48mg; Fibre 2.4g; Sodium 12mg.

Raspberry Trifle

This ever-popular dessert looks wonderful served in a glass bowl so that you can see all the layers. Use fresh or frozen raspberries.

Serves 6–8
175g/6oz trifle sponges, or
  2.5cm/1in cubes of plain
  Victoria sponge or coarsely
  crumbled sponge fingers
60ml/4 tbsp medium sherry
115g/4oz raspberry jam
275g/10oz/1⅔ cups raspberries
450ml/¾ pint/scant 2 cups
  custard, flavoured with 30ml/
  2 tbsp medium or sweet sherry
300ml/½ pint/1¼ cups
  whipping cream
15ml/1tbsp icing (confectioners')
  sugar
toasted flaked (sliced) almonds
  and mint leaves, to decorate

1 Spread half of the sponges, cake cubes or sponge fingers over the bottom of a large serving bowl. (A glass bowl is best for presentation.)

2 Sprinkle half of the sherry over the cake to moisten it. Spoon over half of the jam, dotting it evenly over the cake cubes.

3 Reserve a few raspberries for decoration. Make a layer of half of the remaining raspberries on top.

4 Pour over half of the custard, covering the fruit and cake. Repeat the layers. Cover and chill for at least 2 hours.

5 Before serving, whip the cream with the icing sugar until it forms soft peaks. Spoon the sweetened whipped cream evenly over the top of the custard. To decorate, sprinkle with toasted flaked almonds and arrange the reserved raspberries and the mint leaves on top. Serve as soon as possible.

> **Variation**
> Use other ripe summer fruit such as apricots, peaches, nectarines and strawberries in the trifle, with jam and liqueur to complement the fruit.

Mangoes with Sticky Rice

Glutinous rice is just as good in desserts as in savoury dishes. The delicate fragrance and velvety flesh of mangoes complement the rice especially well. You need to start preparing this dish the day before serving.

Serves 4
115g/4oz/⅔ cup white
  glutinous rice
175ml/6fl oz/¾ cup thick
  coconut milk
40g/1½oz/3 tbsp granulated sugar
pinch of salt
2 ripe mangoes
strips of pared lime rind,
  to decorate

1 Rinse the glutinous rice thoroughly in several changes of cold water, then leave to soak overnight in a bowl of fresh cold water.

2 Drain the rice well and spread it out evenly in a steamer lined with muslin. Cover and steam over a pan of simmering water for about 20 minutes, or until the rice is tender.

3 Reserve 45ml/3 tbsp of the cream from the top of the coconut milk. Pour the remainder into a pan and add the sugar and salt. Heat, stirring constantly, until the sugar has dissolved, then bring to the boil. Remove the pan from the heat, pour the coconut milk into a bowl and leave to cool.

4 Transfer the cooked rice to a bowl and pour over the cooled coconut milk. Stir well; leave to stand for 10–15 minutes. Meanwhile, peel the mangoes, cut the flesh away from the central stones (pits) and cut into slices.

5 Spoon the rice on to individual serving plates. Arrange the mango slices on one side, then drizzle with the reserved coconut cream. Decorate with strips of lime rind and serve.

> **Cook's Tip**
> The thickest part of coconut milk always rises to the top. When you open it, spoon off this top layer to use for serving.

Raspberry Trifle Energy 330Kcal/1382kJ; Protein 5.1g; Carbohydrate 35.9g, of which sugars 29.1g; Fat 17.7g, of which saturates 9.9g; Cholesterol 90mg; Calcium 102mg; Fibre 1.1g; Sodium 59mg.
Mangoes with Rice Energy 200Kcal/846kJ; Protein 3.1g; Carbohydrate 46g, of which sugars 24.3g; Fat 0.8g, of which saturates 0.2g; Cholesterol 0mg; Calcium 32mg; Fibre 2g; Sodium 51mg.

Apricots in Marsala

Rich Marsala creates a beautifully flavoured syrup for the apricots. Serve with amaretti to add to the Italian tone of the dish.

Serves 4

12 apricots
50g/2oz/¼ cup caster (superfine) sugar
300ml/½ pint/1¼ cups Marsala
2 strips pared orange rind
1 vanilla pod (bean), split
250ml/8fl oz/1 cup water
150ml/¼ pint/⅔ cup double (heavy) or whipping cream
15ml/1 tbsp icing (confectioners') sugar
1.5ml/¼ tsp ground cinnamon
150ml/¼ pint/⅔ cup Greek (US strained plain) yogurt
amaretti, to serve

1 Halve and stone (pit) the apricots, then place in a bowl of boiling water for about 30 seconds. Drain well, then slip off their skins.

2 Place the caster sugar, Marsala, orange rind, vanilla pod and water in a pan. Heat gently until the sugar dissolves. Bring to the boil, without stirring, then simmer for 2–3 minutes.

3 Add the apricot halves to the pan and poach for 5–6 minutes, or until just tender. Using a slotted spoon, transfer the apricots to a serving dish.

4 Boil the syrup rapidly until reduced by half, then pour over the apricots and leave to cool. Cover and chill. Remove the orange rind and vanilla pod.

5 Whip the cream with the icing sugar and cinnamon until it forms soft peaks. Gently fold in the yogurt. Spoon the cream into a serving bowl and chill. Serve with the apricots.

Cook's Tip
Make sure that the apricots are completely covered by the syrup so that they don't discolour.

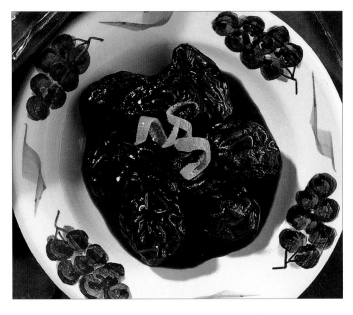

Prunes Poached in Red Wine

Bathed in a lightly aromatic wine sauce, prunes are transformed into something special. Easy to make and quite delicious, this is a particularly useful fruit dessert for the winter time.

Serves 8–10

900g/2lb large pitted prunes
1 unwaxed orange
1 unwaxed lemon
750ml/1¼ pints/3 cups fruity red wine
50g/2oz/¼ cup caster (superfine) sugar, or to taste
1 cinnamon stick
pinch of freshly grated nutmeg
2 or 3 cloves
5ml/1 tsp black peppercorns
1 bay leaf
475ml/16fl oz/2 cups water
strips of orange rind, to decorate (optional)
pouring (half-and-half) cream, to serve

1 Place the prunes in a bowl, cover with water and leave to soak for a few hours.

2 Using a vegetable peeler, pare two or three strips of rind from both the orange and lemon. Squeeze the juice from both and put in a large pan.

3 Add the wine, sugar, spices, peppercorns, bay leaf and strips of rind to the pan with the water.

4 Bring to the boil over a medium heat, stirring occasionally to dissolve the sugar. Drain the prunes and add to the pan. Reduce the heat to low and simmer, covered, for 10–15 minutes until the prunes are tender. Remove from the heat and set aside until cool.

5 Using a slotted spoon, transfer the prunes to a serving dish. Return the cooking liquid to a medium-high heat and bring to the boil. Boil for 5–10 minutes until slightly reduced and syrupy.

6 Pour or strain the hot syrup over the prunes. Cool, then chill in the refrigerator. Serve with cream, decorated with strips of orange rind, if you like.

Apricots in Marsala Energy 448Kcal/1870kJ; Protein 4.2g; Carbohydrate 36g, of which sugars 36g; Fat 24.1g, of which saturates 14.5g; Cholesterol 51mg; Calcium 104mg; Fibre 2.1g; Sodium 41mg.
Prunes in Red Wine Energy 198Kcal/837kJ; Protein 2.4g; Carbohydrate 36g, of which sugars 36g; Fat 0.4g, of which saturates 0g; Cholesterol 0mg; Calcium 39mg; Fibre 5.1g; Sodium 16mg.

Oranges with Caramel Wigs

Naranjas con pelucas is a pretty variation on the normal orange salad. The slightly bitter, caramelized orange rind and syrup sits in perfect harmony with the sweet, juicy oranges.

Serves 6

6 oranges
115g/4oz/generous ½ cup caster (superfine) sugar
120ml/4fl oz/½ cup boiling water, plus extra hot and cold water

1 Using a vegetable peeler, thinly pare the rind off some of the oranges to make at least 12 long strips.

2 Using a sharp knife, peel all the oranges, discarding the pith. and reserving the juice that has collected. Freeze the oranges separately for 30 minutes.

3 Slice the oranges, pile back into their original shape and secure each with a cocktail stick (toothpick). Chill.

4 To make the wigs, simmer the rind for about 5 minutes, drain, rinse, and then repeat. Trim into shape with scissors.

5 Put half the sugar in a small pan and add 15ml/1 tbsp water. Heat gently until the mixture caramelizes, shaking the pan a little if one side starts to brown too fast. As soon as the mixture colours, dip the bottom of the pan into cold water. Add 30ml/2 tbsp hot water and the orange rind to the caramel, then stir until the caramel dissolves. Turn the rind on to a plate to cool.

6 Make a caramel syrup for serving. Put the remaining sugar in a small pan with 15ml/1 tbsp water, and make caramel as before. When it has coloured nicely, stand well back, pour in the boiling water and stir with a wooden spoon to dissolve. Add the reserved orange juice and pour into a serving jug (pitcher).

7 To serve, arrange the orange strips in a criss-cross pattern on top of each orange. Remove the cocktail sticks and pour a little caramel syrup round the base of each orange.

Bananas with Lime & Cardamom Sauce

Serve these bananas solo, with ice cream, or spoon them over folded crêpes.

Serves 4

6 small bananas
50g/2oz/¼ cup butter
seeds from 4 cardamom pods, crushed
50g/2oz/½ cup flaked (sliced) almonds
thinly pared rind and juice of 2 limes
50g/2oz/¼ cup light muscovado (brown) sugar
30ml/2 tbsp dark rum
vanilla ice cream, to serve

1 Peel the bananas and cut them in half lengthways. Heat half the butter in a large frying pan. Add half the bananas, and cook until the undersides are golden. Turn carefully, using a fish slice. Cook until golden.

2 As they cook, transfer the bananas to a heatproof serving dish. Cook the remaining bananas in the same way.

3 Melt the remaining butter, then add the cardamom seeds and almonds. Cook, stirring until golden.

4 Stir in the lime rind and juice, then the sugar. Cook, stirring, until the mixture is smooth and also slightly reduced. Stir in the rum. Pour the sauce over the bananas and allow to cool. Serve with the vanilla ice cream.

Cook's Tip
Use green cardamom pods, split open, and scrape out the black seeds, then crush to help release the aromatic flavour.

Variation
Use orange or pineapple juice in place of the rum, if you prefer.

Oranges Energy 129Kcal/552kJ; Protein 1.6g; Carbohydrate 32.5g, of which sugars 32.5g; Fat 0.1g, of which saturates 0g; Cholesterol 0mg; Calcium 75mg; Fibre 2.3g; Sodium 8mg.
Bananas Energy 350Kcal/1462kJ; Protein 4.2g; Carbohydrate 41.9g, of which sugars 38.8g; Fat 17.6g, of which saturates 7.2g; Cholesterol 27mg; Calcium 46mg; Fibre 2.3g; Sodium 80mg.

Clementines in Cinnamon Caramel

The combination of sweet yet sharp clementines and caramel sauce, flavoured with a hint of spice, is divine. Serve with thick yogurt or crème fraîche to make a delicious dessert for family and friends.

Serves 4–6
8–12 clementines
225g/8oz/1 cup granulated sugar
300ml/½ pint/1¼ cups warm water
2 cinnamon sticks
30ml/2 tbsp orange-flavoured liqueur
25g/1oz/¼ cup shelled pistachio nuts

1 Using a vegetable peeler, pare the rind from two clementines, and cut it into fine strips. Set aside.

2 Peel the clementines, removing all the pith but keeping them intact. Put the fruits in a serving bowl.

3 Gently heat the sugar in a pan until it melts and turns a rich golden brown. Immediately turn off the heat.

4 Cover your hand with a dish towel and pour in the warm water (the mixture will bubble violently). Bring slowly to the boil, stirring until the caramel has dissolved. Add the shredded rind and whole cinnamon sticks, then simmer for 5 minutes. Stir in the orange-flavoured liqueur.

5 Leave the syrup to cool for about 10 minutes, then pour over the clementines. Cover the bowl and chill for several hours or overnight.

6 Blanch the pistachios in boiling water. Drain, cool and remove the dark outer skins. Scatter over the clementines and serve.

Cook's Tip
Watch out when you add the water as the mixture will splutter.

Star Anise Fruits with Coconut Jelly

This simple yet rather unusual Eastern-influenced dessert is sure to impress the most jaded of palates. It is best served after any oriental-style meal, with plenty of extra exotic fruit.

Serves 4
For the coconut jelly
250ml/8fl oz/1 cup water
75g/3oz/6 tbsp caster (superfine) sugar
15ml/1 tbsp powdered gelatine
400ml/14fl oz/1⅔ cups coconut milk

For the syrup and fruit
250ml/8fl oz/1 cup water
3 star anise
50g/2oz/¼ cup caster (superfine) sugar
1 star fruit, sliced
12 lychees, peeled and stoned (pitted)
115g/4oz/1 cup blackberries

1 Pour the water into a pan and add the caster sugar. Heat gently until the sugar has dissolved.

2 Sprinkle over the gelatine and continue to heat the mixture gently until the gelatine has dissolved, stirring occasionally.

3 Stir the coconut milk into the sugar syrup, remove from the heat and set aside to cool.

4 Grease an 18cm/7in square cake tin (pan). Line with clear film (plastic wrap). Carefully pour the coconut milk mixture into the lined cake tin and chill to set.

5 Make the syrup. Combine the water, star anise and sugar in a pan. Bring to the boil, stirring, then lower the heat and simmer for about 10–12 minutes or until syrupy.

6 Place the fruit in a heatproof bowl and pour over the hot syrup. Cool, then chill.

7 To serve, cut the coconut jelly into diamond shapes and remove from the tin. Arrange the coconut jelly diamonds on individual plates, adding a few of the fruits and their syrup to each portion.

Clementines Energy 216Kcal/915kJ; Protein 1.7g; Carbohydrate 48.1g, of which sugars 48g; Fat 2.4g, of which saturates 0.3g; Cholesterol 0mg; Calcium 50mg; Fibre 1.2g; Sodium 28mg.
Star Anise Fruits Energy 184Kcal/787kJ; Protein 1.2g; Carbohydrate 47g, of which sugars 47g; Fat 0.4g, of which saturates 0.2g; Cholesterol 0mg; Calcium 61mg; Fibre 1.5g; Sodium 113mg.

Summer Pudding

Unbelievably simple to make and totally delicious, this is a real warm-weather classic. It's also a productive way of using up leftover bread.

Serves 4
about 8 slices white bread, at least one day old
800g/1¾lb mixed summer fruits
about 25g/1oz/2 tbsp granulated sugar
30ml/2 tbsp water

1 Remove the crusts from the bread. Cut a round from one slice of bread to fit in the base of a 1.2 litre/2 pint/5 cup round heatproof bowl and place in position. Cut strips of bread about 5cm/2in wide and use to line the sides of the bowl, overlapping the strips as you work.

2 Gently heat the fruit, sugar and the water in a large heavy pan, shaking the pan occasionally, until the juices begin to run.

3 Reserve about 45ml/3 tbsp fruit juice, then spoon the fruit and remaining juice into the prepared bowl, taking care not to dislodge the bread lining.

4 Cut the remaining bread to fit entirely over the fruit. Stand the bowl on a plate and cover with a saucer or small plate that will just fit inside the top of the bowl. Place a heavy weight on top. Chill the pudding and the reserved fruit juice overnight.

5 Run a knife carefully around the inside of the bowl rim, then invert the pudding on to a cold serving plate. Pour over the reserved juice, making sure that all the bread is completely covered, and serve.

Cook's Tips
• *Use a good mix of summer fruits for this pudding – red- and blackcurrants, raspberries, strawberries and loganberries.*
• *Summer pudding freezes well so make an extra one to enjoy during the winter.*

Autumn Pudding

As its name suggests, this is a tasty seasonal variation of summer pudding, using apples, blackberries and plums – a great combination.

Serves 6
10 slices white or brown bread, at least one day old
1 cooking apple, peeled, cored and sliced
225g/8oz ripe red plums, halved and stoned (pitted)
225g/8oz blackberries
75g/3oz/6 tbsp caster (superfine) sugar
60ml/4 tbsp water
natural (plain) yogurt or Greek (US strained plain) yogurt, to serve

1 Remove the crusts from the bread. Cut a round from one slice of bread to fit in the base of a 1.2 litre/2 pint/5 cup round heatproof bowl and place in position.

2 Cut the remaining slices of bread in half and use to line the bowl, overlapping the pieces as you work. Save some pieces of bread for the top.

3 Place the apple, plums, blackberries, caster sugar and the water in a pan. Heat gently until the sugar dissolves, then simmer for 10 minutes, until soft. Remove from the heat.

4 Spoon the fruit into the bread-lined bowl, reserving the juice. Cut the remaining bread to fit entirely over the fruit, then gently spoon over the reserved fruit juice.

5 Stand the bowl on a plate and cover with a saucer or small plate that will just fit inside the top of the bowl. Place a heavy weight on top. Chill the pudding overnight. Turn out on to a serving plate and serve with natural or Greek yogurt.

Cook's Tip
Choose good-quality bread, with slices at least 5mm/¼in thick so that it supports the fruit when the pudding is turned out.

Ruby Plum Mousse

Red plums and ruby port give this lovely mousse its delicate flavour. The dessert is topped with a scattering of chopped pistachios, adding a splash of colour and interest.

Serves 6
450g/1lb ripe red plums
40g/1½oz/3 tbsp granulated sugar
75ml/5 tbsp water
60ml/4 tbsp ruby port
15ml/1 tbsp/1 sachet powdered gelatine
3 eggs, separated
115g/4oz/generous ½ cup caster (superfine) sugar
150ml/¼ pint/⅔ cup double (heavy) cream
skinned and chopped pistachio nuts, to decorate

1 Place the plums and granulated sugar in a pan with 30ml/2 tbsp water. Cook the fruit and sugar over a low heat until the fruit has softened.

2 Press the fruit through a sieve (strainer) in order to remove the stones (pits) and skins. Leave the fruit to cool, and then stir in the port.

3 Put the remaining water in a small bowl, sprinkle over the gelatine and leave to soften.

4 Stand the bowl in a pan of hot water and leave until dissolved. Stir into the plum purée.

5 Place the egg yolks and caster sugar in a bowl and whisk until thick and mousse-like.

6 Fold in the plum purée, then whip the cream and fold in gently.

7 Whisk the egg whites until they hold stiff peaks, then carefully fold in using a metal spoon.

8 Divide among six glasses and chill until set.

9 To serve, decorate the plum mousses with a sprinkling of chopped pistachio nuts.

Mango & Lime Fool

Canned mangoes are used here for convenience, but the dish tastes even better if made with fresh ones. Choose a variety like the voluptuous Alphonso mango, which is wonderfully fragrant and tastes indescribably delicious.

Serves 4
400g/14oz can sliced mango
grated rind of 1 lime
juice of ½ lime
150ml/¼ pint/⅔ cup double (heavy) cream
90ml/6 tbsp Greek (US strained plain) yogurt
fresh mango slices, to decorate (optional)

1 Drain the canned mango slices and put them in the bowl of a food processor. Add the grated lime rind and the lime juice. Process until the mixture forms a smooth purée. Alternatively, mash the mango slices with a potato masher, then press through a sieve (strainer) into a bowl with the back of a wooden spoon. Stir in the lime rind and juice.

2 Pour the cream into a mixing bowl and add the yogurt. Whisk until the mixture is thick and then quickly whisk in the mango mixture.

3 Spoon into tall glasses and chill for 1–2 hours. Just before serving, decorate each glass with fresh mango slices, if you like.

Cook's Tip
When mixing the cream and yogurt mixture with the mango purée, whisk just enough to combine, so as not to lose the lightness of the whipped cream mixture. If you prefer, fold the mixtures together lightly, so that the fool is rippled.

Variation
This fool can also be made with canned apricots, using orange rind and juice in place of the lime.

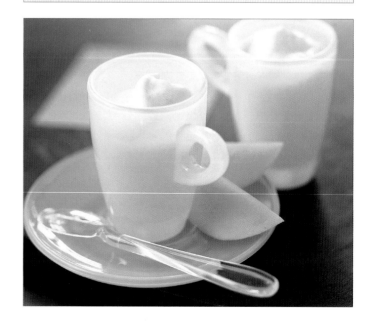

Plum Mousse Energy 309Kcal/1293kJ; Protein 4.1g; Carbohydrate 36.1g, of which sugars 36.1g; Fat 16.3g, of which saturates 9.1g; Cholesterol 129mg; Calcium 51mg; Fibre 1.2g; Sodium 44mg.
Mango & Lime Fool Energy 289Kcal/1203kJ; Protein 2.4g; Carbohydrate 21.4g, of which sugars 21.3g; Fat 22.4g, of which saturates 13.7g; Cholesterol 51mg; Calcium 62mg; Fibre 0.7g; Sodium 27mg.

Gooseberry & Elderflower Fool

Gooseberries and elderflowers are a match made in heaven, each bringing out the flavour of the other. Serve with amaretti or other dessert biscuits for dipping.

Serves 6
450g/1lb/4 cups gooseberries, trimmed
30ml/2 tbsp water
50–75g/2–3oz/¼–⅓ cup caster (superfine) sugar
30ml/2 tbsp elderflower cordial
400g/14oz fresh ready-made custard
green food colouring (optional)
300ml/½ pint/1¼ cups double (heavy) cream
crushed amaretti, to decorate

1 Put the gooseberries and water in a pan. Cover and cook for 5–6 minutes or until the berries pop open.

2 Add the sugar and elderflower cordial to the gooseberries, then stir vigorously or mash until the fruit forms a pulp. Remove the pan from the heat, spoon the gooseberry pulp into a bowl and set aside to cool.

3 Stir the custard into the fruit. Add a few drops of food colouring, if using. Whip the cream to soft peaks, then fold it into the mixture and chill. Serve the fool in dessert glasses, decorated with crushed amaretti, and accompanied by amaretti.

Cook's Tip
In the summer, you can always make your own elderflower cordial by leaving freshly picked elderflower heads to infuse in water with sugar and lemon for 24 hours. Use immediately.

Variation
Use puréed raspberries, sweetened to taste, instead of the cooked gooseberries and omit the elderflower cordial.

Clementine Jelly

Jelly isn't only for children: this adult version has a clean fruity taste and can be made extra special by adding a dash of white rum or Cointreau.

Serves 4
12 clementines
clear grape juice (see method for amount)
15ml/1 tbsp powdered gelatine
25g/1oz/2 tbsp caster (superfine) sugar
whipped cream, to decorate

1 Squeeze the juice from eight of the clementines and pour into a jug (pitcher). Make up to 600ml/1 pint/2½ cups with the grape juice, then strain the mixture through a sieve (strainer).

2 Pour half the juice mixture into a pan. Sprinkle the gelatine on top, leave to stand for 5 minutes, then heat gently until the gelatine has completely dissolved. Stir in the sugar, then the remaining juice; set aside.

3 Pare the rind very thinly from the remaining fruit and set it aside. Using a small sharp knife, cut between the membrane and fruit to separate the citrus segments. Discard the membrane and white pith.

4 Place half the segments in four dessert glasses and cover with some of the liquid fruit jelly. Leave in the refrigerator to set.

5 When the jellies are set, arrange the remaining segments on top. Carefully pour over the remaining liquid jelly and chill until set. Cut the pared clementine rind into fine shreds. Serve the jellies topped with a generous spoonful of whipped cream scattered with clementine rind shreds.

Variation
Use four ruby grapefruit instead of clementines, if you prefer. Squeeze the juice from half of them and segment the rest, discarding any bitter white pith.

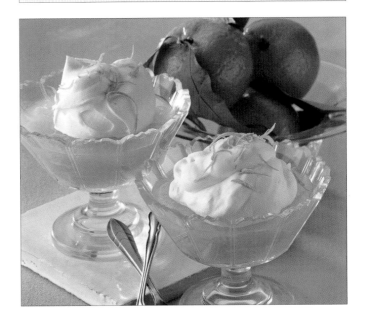

Gooseberry Fool Energy 333Kcal/1381kJ; Protein 3.4g; Carbohydrate 15.5g, of which sugars 13.1g; Fat 28.4g, of which saturates 16.7g; Cholesterol 70mg; Calcium 107mg; Fibre 1.9g; Sodium 40mg.
Clementine Jelly Energy 97Kcal/414kJ; Protein 1.3g; Carbohydrate 24.1g, of which sugars 24.1g; Fat 0.2g, of which saturates 0g; Cholesterol 0mg; Calcium 51mg; Fibre 1.5g; Sodium 9mg.

Frozen French Raspberry Mousse

Fill the centre of this lovely
French dessert with extra
raspberries, if you like.

Serves 6
350g/12oz/2 cups raspberries
40g/1½oz/3 tbsp icing
   (confectioners') sugar
2 egg whites

1.5ml/¼ tsp cream of tartar
90g/3½oz/scant ½ cup
   granulated sugar
25ml/1½ tbsp lemon juice
250ml/8fl oz/1 cup whipping
   cream
15ml/1 tbsp framboise or Kirsch
fresh mint leaves, to decorate

1 Put the raspberries in a food processor fitted with a metal blade and process until smooth. Press through a sieve (strainer).

2 Pour about a third of the purée into a small bowl, stir in the icing sugar, then cover and chill. Reserve the remaining purée for the mousse.

3 Half-fill a medium pan with hot water and place over a low heat (do not allow the water to boil). Combine the egg whites, cream of tartar, sugar and lemon juice in a heatproof bowl that just fits into the pan without touching the water. Using an electric whisk, beat at medium-high speed until the beaters leave tracks on the base of the bowl, then beat at high speed for about 7 minutes until the mixture is very thick and forms stiff peaks.

4 Remove the bowl from the pan and continue beating the egg white mixture for a further 2–3 minutes until it is cool. Fold in the reserved raspberry purée.

5 Whip the cream until it forms soft peaks and fold gently into the raspberry mixture with the framboise or Kirsch. Spoon into a 1.4 litre/2½ pint/6 cup ring mould, then cover and freeze for at least 4 hours or overnight.

6 To unmould, dip the mould in warm water for about 5 seconds and turn the mousse out on to a plate. Decorate with mint sprigs and serve with the sweetened raspberry purée.

Peach & Ginger Pashka

A low-fat version of the
Russian Easter favourite –
a glorious cheese dessert
flavoured with peaches and
preserved stem ginger.

Serves 4
350g/12oz/1½ cups low-fat
   cottage cheese
2 ripe peaches or nectarines
90g/3½oz/scant ½ cup low-fat
   natural (plain) yogurt

2 pieces preserved stem ginger in
   syrup, drained and chopped,
   plus 30ml/2 tbsp syrup from
   the jar
2.5ml/½ tsp vanilla extract

To decorate
1 peach or nectarine, peeled and
   sliced
10ml/2 tsp slivered almonds,
   toasted

1 Drain the cottage cheese and rub it through a fine sieve (strainer) into a bowl. Remove the stones (pits) from the peaches or nectarines and roughly chop.

2 Mix together the chopped peaches or nectarines in a large bowl with the low-fat cottage cheese, yogurt, preserved stem ginger, syrup and vanilla extract.

3 Line a new, clean flower pot or a sieve (strainer) with a piece of clean, fine cloth, such as muslin (cheesecloth).

4 Add the cheese mixture and wrap over the cloth to cover. Place a saucer on top and weigh down. Stand over a bowl in a cool place and leave to drain overnight.

5 To serve, unwrap the cloth and turn the pashka out on to a serving plate. Decorate the pashka with peach or nectarine slices and toasted almonds.

> **Cook's Tip**
> *Rather than making one large pashka, line four to six cups or ramekins with the clean cloth or muslin (cheesecloth) and divide the mixture evenly among them.*

Raspberry Mousse Energy 271Kcal/1135kJ; Protein 2.7g; Carbohydrate 27.3g, of which sugars 27.3g; Fat 17g, of which saturates 10.6g; Cholesterol 44mg; Calcium 51mg; Fibre 1.5g; Sodium 34mg.
Pashka Energy 157Kcal/660kJ; Protein 13.3g; Carbohydrate 14.7g, of which sugars 14.6g; Fat 5.1g, of which saturates 2.3g; Cholesterol 14mg; Calcium 165mg; Fibre 1g; Sodium 302mg.

Chocolate Mandarin Trifle

Rich chocolate custard is combined with mandarin oranges to make a trifle that is too tempting to resist.

Serves 6–8
4 trifle sponges
14 amaretti
60ml/4 tbsp Amaretto di Saronno
   or sweet sherry
8 mandarin oranges

For the custard
200g/7oz plain (semisweet)
   chocolate, broken into squares
25g/1oz/2 tbsp cornflour
   (cornstarch) or custard powder
25g/1oz/2 tbsp caster
   (superfine) sugar
2 egg yolks
200ml/7fl oz/scant 1 cup milk
250g/9oz/generous 1 cup
   mascarpone

For the topping
250g/9oz/generous 1 cup
   mascarpone or fromage frais
chocolate shapes
mandarin slices

1 Break up the trifle sponges and place them in a large glass serving dish. Crumble the amaretti over and then sprinkle with Amaretto or sweet sherry.

2 Squeeze the juice from two of the mandarins and sprinkle into the dish. Segment the rest and put in the dish.

3 Make the custard. Melt the chocolate in a heatproof bowl over hot water. In a separate bowl, mix the cornflour or custard powder, sugar and egg yolks to a smooth paste.

4 Heat the milk in a small pan until almost boiling, then pour in a steady stream on to the egg yolk mixture, stirring constantly. Return to the pan and stir over a low heat until the custard has thickened slightly and is smooth.

5 Stir in the mascarpone until melted, then add the melted chocolate; mix well. Spread over the trifle, cool, then chill to set.

6 To finish, spread the mascarpone or fromage frais over the custard, then decorate with chocolate shapes and the remaining mandarin slices just before serving.

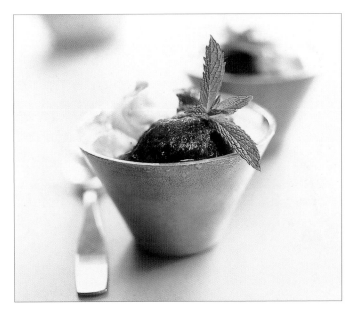

Blackcurrant & Meringue Trifles

Trifle with a twist, this quick and easy dessert is made using crushed meringues, cream and sorbet. Served in individual dishes, it is suitable for any occasion.

Serves 6
350ml/12fl oz/1½ cups
   blackcurrant sorbet
3 bought meringues
several sprigs of fresh mint, plus
   extra mint sprigs, to decorate
30ml/2 tbsp icing (confectioners')
   sugar
20ml/4 tsp freshly squeezed
   lemon juice
300ml/½ pint/1¼ cups double
   (heavy) or whipping cream
90ml/6 tbsp Greek (US strained
   plain) yogurt

1 Remove the blackcurrant sorbet from the freezer for about 20 minutes to soften slightly. Roughly break the meringues into small pieces.

2 Chop the mint finely and put it into a bowl. Add the icing sugar, lemon juice and cream. Whip until the mixture just holds its shape. Stir in the Greek yogurt, then carefully fold in the crushed meringues.

3 Spoon a little of the cream mixture into six small, deep dishes or glasses. Add layers of sorbet and cream mixture, ending with cream mixture. Decorate with mint sprigs.

Cook's Tip
The number this will serve will depend on the size of the dishes used. If you opt for large, bowl-shaped glasses, the mixture will probably serve four.

Variation
Leave out the chopped mint, if you prefer. The blackcurrant sorbet gives a good colour and flavour contrast to the cream mixture, but you could use any other flavourful sorbet instead.

Choc. Mandarin Energy 569Kcal/2394kJ; Protein 12.5g; Carbohydrate 80.3g, of which sugars 61.3g; Fat 23.1g, of which saturates 12.8g; Cholesterol 135mg; Calcium 162mg; Fibre 2.9g; Sodium 115mg.
Blackcurrant & Meringue Energy 405Kcal/1687kJ; Protein 2.8g; Carbohydrate 36.9g, of which sugars 36g; Fat 28.6g, of which saturates 17.5g; Cholesterol 69mg; Calcium 56mg; Fibre 0g; Sodium 47mg.

Summer Fruit Salad Ice Cream

A combination of yogurt and luscious soft fruits, this mouthwatering ice cream makes a fresh, low-fat treat for summer days.

Serves 6
900g/2lb/6 cups mixed soft
   summer fruit, such as
   raspberries, strawberries,
   blackcurrants or redcurrants

2 eggs
250ml/8fl oz/1 cup low-fat
   Greek (US strained
   plain) yogurt
175ml/6fl oz/³⁄4 cup red
   grape juice
15ml/1 tbsp powdered gelatine

1 Reserve half the fruit for the decoration; purée the rest in a food processor, then strain it over a bowl to make a smooth purée.

2 Separate the eggs and whisk the yolks and the yogurt into the fruit purée.

3 Heat the grape juice until almost boiling, then remove it from the heat. Sprinkle the gelatine over the grape juice and stir to dissolve the gelatine completely.

4 Whisk the dissolved gelatine mixture into the fruit purée. Cool, then pour the mixture into a freezer container. Freeze until half-frozen and slushy in consistency.

5 Whisk the egg whites in a grease-free bowl until stiff. Quickly fold them into the half-frozen mixture.

6 Return to the freezer and freeze until almost firm. To serve, scoop into dishes and decorate with the reserved soft fruits.

Cook's Tip
Red grape juice has a good flavour and improves the colour of the ice, but if it is not available, use cranberry, apple or orange juice instead.

Christmas Cranberry Bombe

This healthy alternative to Christmas pudding is light and low in fat, but still very festive and luxurious.

Serves 6
250ml/8fl oz/1 cup buttermilk
60ml/4 tbsp half-fat crème fraîche
1 vanilla pod (bean)
2 eggs
30ml/2 tbsp clear honey
30ml/2 tbsp chopped angelica
30ml/2 tbsp mixed (candied) peel

10ml/2 tsp flaked (sliced)
   almonds, toasted

For the sorbet centre
175g/6oz/1¹⁄2 cups fresh or
   frozen cranberries
150ml/¹⁄4 pint/²⁄3 cup fresh
   orange juice
finely grated rind of ¹⁄2 orange
2.5ml/¹⁄2 tsp mixed spice (apple
   pie spice)
50g/2oz/¹⁄4 cup golden
   caster (superfine) sugar

1 Heat the buttermilk, crème fraîche and vanilla pod in a pan until the mixture is almost boiling. Remove the vanilla pod.

2 Place the eggs in a heatproof bowl over a pan of hot water and whisk until they are pale and thick. Pour in the heated buttermilk in a thin stream, whisking hard. Continue whisking over the hot water until the mixture thickens slightly.

3 Whisk in the honey and leave to cool. Spoon the mixture into a freezer container and freeze until slushy, then turn into a bowl and stir in the chopped angelica, mixed peel and almonds. Spoon into a 1.2 litre/2 pint/5 cup freezerproof round bowl and hollow out the centre. Freeze until firm.

4 Meanwhile, make the sorbet centre. Put the cranberries, orange juice, rind and spice in a pan and cook gently until the cranberries are soft. Set some cranberries aside for decorating. Add the sugar to the rest, then purée in a food processor until almost smooth, but still with some texture. Leave to cool.

5 Fill the hollowed-out centre of the bombe with the cranberry mixture, smooth over and freeze until firm. To serve, allow to soften slightly at room temperature, then turn out and serve in slices, decorated with the reserved cranberries.

Fruit Salad Ice Cream Energy 134Kcal/558kJ; Protein 5.8g; Carbohydrate 14.4g, of which sugars 14.3g; Fat 6.3g, of which saturates 3.3g; Cholesterol 70mg; Calcium 92mg; Fibre 1.7g; Sodium 62mg.
Cranberry Bombe Energy 147Kcal/622kJ; Protein 4.6g; Carbohydrate 22.7g, of which sugars 22.5g; Fat 5g, of which saturates 1.7g; Cholesterol 65mg; Calcium 91mg; Fibre 0.9g; Sodium 64mg.

Frozen Apple & Blackberry Terrine

This pretty autumn fruit terrine is frozen so that you can enjoy a healthy dessert at any time of the year.

Serves 6
450g/1lb cooking or eating apples
300ml/½ pint/1¼ cups
   sweet (hard) cider
15ml/1 tbsp clear honey
5ml/1 tsp pure vanilla extract
200g/7oz/scant 2 cups fresh or
   frozen and thawed blackberries
15ml/1 tbsp powdered gelatine
2 egg whites
fresh apple slices and
   blackberries, to decorate

1 Peel, core and chop the apples and place them in a pan with half the cider. Bring the cider to the boil, then lower the heat, cover the pan and let the apples simmer gently until tender.

2 Transfer the apples to a food processor and process them to a smooth purée. Stir in the honey and vanilla extract. Add half the blackberries to half the apple purée, and process again until smooth. Press through a sieve (strainer) to remove the seeds.

3 Heat the remaining cider until almost boiling, then sprinkle the gelatine over and stir until the gelatine has dissolved completely. Add half the gelatine mixture to the apple purée and half to the blackberry and apple purée.

4 Leave both purées to cool until almost set. Whisk the egg whites until they are stiff. Quickly fold them into the apple purée. Remove half the purée to another bowl. Stir the remaining whole blackberries into half the apple purée, and then transfer this to a 1.75 litre/3 pint/7½ cup loaf tin (pan), packing it down firmly.

5 Top with the blackberry purée and spread it evenly. Finally, add a layer of the plain apple purée and smooth it evenly. If necessary, freeze each layer until firm before adding the next.

6 Freeze until firm. To serve, remove from the freezer and allow to stand at room temperature for about 20 minutes to soften. Serve in slices, decorated with apple slices and blackberries.

Plum & Port Sorbet

A melt-in-the-mouth sorbet with a wonderful taste and colour, this fat-free ice is a refreshing way to round off any meal.

Serves 4–6
900g/2lb ripe red plums, halved
   and stoned (pitted)
75g/3oz/6 tbsp caster
   (superfine) sugar
45ml/3 tbsp water
45ml/3 tbsp ruby port or red wine
crisp biscuits (cookies), to serve
   (optional)

1 Place the plums in a pan with the sugar and the water. Stir over a low heat until the sugar has melted, then cover and simmer gently for about 5 minutes, until the fruit is soft.

2 Turn the plum mixture into a blender or food processor and purée until smooth, then stir in the port. Allow to cool completely, then transfer to a freezer container and freeze until firm round the edges.

3 Remove from the freezer and process in the food processor or beat with an electric whisk to break up the ice crystals. Put back in the freezer and freeze until solid.

4 Before serving, allow the sorbet to stand for 15–20 minutes until softened slightly, then scoop on to individual dishes and serve with crisp biscuits, if you like.

> **Cook's Tip**
> *If you prefer not to use alcohol, leave out the port and use fresh red grape juice instead for an equally delicious taste.*

> **Variation**
> *Use redcurrants and strawberries instead of the plums, pressing them through a sieve (strainer) after puréeing.*

Apple & Blackberry Terrine Energy 67Kcal/283kJ; Protein 1.5g; Carbohydrate 12.4g, of which sugars 12.4g; Fat 0.2g, of which saturates 0g; Cholesterol 0mg; Calcium 21mg; Fibre 2.2g; Sodium 26mg.
Plum & Port Sorbet Energy 115Kcal/492kJ; Protein 1g; Carbohydrate 27.2g, of which sugars 27.2g; Fat 0.2g, of which saturates 0g; Cholesterol 0mg; Calcium 27mg; Fibre 2.4g; Sodium 4mg.

Rich Blackcurrant Coulis

A simple decorative trick makes these low-fat fruity desserts look stunning.

Serves 6-8
6 sheets leaf gelatine
475ml/16fl oz/2 cups water
450g/1lb/4 cups blackcurrants

225g/8oz/1 cup caster
  (superfine) sugar
150ml/¼ pint/⅔ cup ruby port
30ml/2 tbsp crème de cassis
120ml/4fl oz/½ cup single (light)
  cream, to decorate

1 In a small bowl, soak the gelatine in 75ml/5 tbsp of the water until soft. Place the blackcurrants, sugar and 300ml/½ pint/1¼ cups of the remaining water in a large pan. Bring to the boil, lower the heat and simmer for 20 minutes.

2 Strain, reserving the cooking liquid in a large jug (pitcher). Put half the blackcurrants in a bowl and pour over 60ml/4 tbsp of the reserved cooking liquid. (Freeze the remaining blackcurrants for another day.) Set the bowl and jug aside.

3 Squeeze the water out of the gelatine and place in a small pan with the port, cassis and remaining water. Heat gently to dissolve the gelatine but do not allow the mixture to boil. Pour the gelatine mixture into the jug of blackcurrant liquid, stirring until well mixed.

4 Run 6–8 jelly moulds under cold water, drain and place in a roasting pan. Fill with the port mixture. Chill for at least 6 hours until set. Turn the bowl of blackcurrants into a food processor, purée until smooth, then pass through a fine sieve (strainer) to make the coulis; adjust the sweetness.

5 Run a fine knife around each jelly. Dip each mould in hot water for 5–10 seconds, then turn the jelly out on to your hand. Place on a serving plate and spoon the coulis around the jelly.

6 To decorate, drop a little cream at intervals on to the coulis. Draw a cocktail stick (toothpick) through the cream dots, dragging each into a heart shape. Serve the desserts immediately.

Apple Foam with Blackberries

A light dessert, with a good contrast in flavour, texture and colour – weight watchers will love it.

Serves 4
225g/8oz blackberries
150ml/¼ pint/⅔ cup clear
  apple juice
5ml/1 tsp powdered gelatine
15ml/1 tbsp clear honey
2 egg whites

1 Place the blackberries in a pan with 60ml/4 tbsp of the apple juice and heat gently until the fruit is soft. Remove from the heat, cool and chill.

2 Sprinkle the gelatine over the remaining apple juice in another pan. Leave to soak for 5 minutes until spongy, then place over a low heat until the gelatine has completely dissolved. Stir in the honey.

3 Whisk the egg whites in a bowl until they hold stiff peaks. Continue whisking hard while gradually pouring in the hot gelatine mixture, until well mixed.

4 Quickly spoon the foam into rough mounds on individual plates. Chill in the refrigerator, then serve with the blackberries and juice spooned around the foam.

Cook's Tips
• Make sure that you dissolve the gelatine over a very low heat. It must not boil, or it will lose its setting ability.
• The egg white foam acts here as a flavourful, low-fat alternative to flavoured cream.

Variation
Any seasonal soft fruit can be used to accompany the apple foam if blackberries are not available.

Blackcurrant Coulis Energy 202Kcal/855kJ; Protein 1.3g; Carbohydrate 37g, of which sugars 37g; Fat 3.6g, of which saturates 2.3g; Cholesterol 10mg; Calcium 66mg; Fibre 2g; Sodium 10mg.
Apple Foam with Blackberries Energy 45Kcal/191kJ; Protein 2g; Carbohydrate 9.5g, of which sugars 9.5g; Fat 0.2g, of which saturates 0g; Cholesterol 0mg; Calcium 27mg; Fibre 1.8g; Sodium 33mg.

Fluffy Banana & Pineapple Mousse

This delicious mousse looks very impressive but is in fact easy to make, especially with a food processor. As an added bonus, it's surprisingly low in fat, so everyone can indulge in the dessert without feeling guilty.

Serves 6

2 ripe bananas
225g/8oz/1 cup cottage cheese
425g/15oz can pineapple chunks
   or pieces in juice
15ml/1 tbsp/1 sachet powdered
   gelatine
2 egg whites

1 Tie a double band of non-stick baking parchment around a 600ml/1 pint/2½ cup soufflé dish, so that it comes 5cm/2in above the rim.

2 Peel and chop one banana and place it in a blender or food processor with the cottage cheese. Process until smooth.

3 Drain the pineapple, reserving the juice. Reserve a few pieces or chunks of pineapple for decoration and add the rest to the mixture in the blender or food processor and process for a few seconds until finely chopped.

4 Dissolve the gelatine in 60ml/4 tbsp of the reserved pineapple juice. Stir the gelatine quickly into the fruit mixture.

5 Whisk the egg whites until they hold soft peaks and fold them into the mixture. Turn the mousse mixture into the prepared dish, smooth the surface and chill until set.

6 When the mousse is set, carefully remove the paper collar. Slice the remaining banana and use with the pineapple to decorate the mousse. Serve immediately.

> **Cook's Tip**
> *To make the preparation of this mousse even simpler, use a 1 litre/1¾ pint/4 cup serving dish, which will hold all the mixture without a paper collar.*

Minted Raspberry Bavarois

A sophisticated dessert that is low in fat, yet looks and tastes delectable.

Serves 6

450g/1lb/2⅔ cups fresh or frozen
   and thawed raspberries
25g/1oz/2 tbsp icing
   (confectioners') sugar
30ml/2 tbsp lemon juice

15ml/1 tbsp finely chopped
   fresh mint
30ml/2 tbsp/2 sachets powdered
   gelatine
75ml/5 tbsp boiling water
300ml/½ pint/1¼ cups custard,
   made with skimmed milk
250g/9oz/generous 1 cup Greek
   (US strained plain) yogurt
fresh mint sprigs, to decorate

1 Reserve a few raspberries for decoration. Place the raspberries, icing sugar and lemon juice in a blender or food processor and process until smooth.

2 Press the purée through a sieve (strainer) to remove the raspberry seeds. Add the mint. You should have about 600ml/1 pint/2½ cups of purée.

3 Sprinkle 5ml/1 tsp of the gelatine over 30ml/2 tbsp of boiling water and stir until the gelatine has dissolved. Stir into 150ml/¼ pint/⅔ cup of the fruit purée.

4 Pour this jelly into a 1 litre/1¾ pint/4 cup mould, and leave the mould to chill in the refrigerator until the jelly is just on the point of setting. Tip the tin to swirl the setting jelly around the sides, and then leave to chill until the jelly has set completely.

5 Stir the remaining fruit purée into the custard and yogurt. Dissolve the rest of the gelatine in 45ml/3 tbsp of boiling water and stir it in quickly.

6 Pour the raspberry custard into the mould and leave it to chill until it has set completely.

7 To serve, dip the mould quickly into hot water and then turn it out into a serving dish. Decorate the bavarois with the reserved raspberries and the mint sprigs.

Fluffy Mousse Energy 102Kcal/431kJ; Protein 6.2g; Carbohydrate 16.4g, of which sugars 15.7g; Fat 1.6g, of which saturates 0.9g; Cholesterol 6mg; Calcium 56mg; Fibre 0.7g; Sodium 134mg.
Raspb. Bavarois Energy 141Kcal/597kJ; Protein 5.1g; Carbohydrate 19.2g, of which sugars 17.5g; Fat 5.4g, of which saturates 2.2g; Cholesterol 1mg; Calcium 130mg; Fibre 1.9g; Sodium 53mg.

Date & Tofu Ice

All you sceptics who claim to hate tofu, prepare to be converted by this creamy date and apple ice cream. Generously spiced with cinnamon, it not only tastes good but is packed with soya protein, contains no added sugar, is low in fat and free from all dairy products.

Serves 4
250g/9oz/1½ cups stoned (pitted) dates
600ml/1 pint/2½ cups apple juice
5ml/1 tsp ground cinnamon
285g/10½oz pack chilled tofu, drained and cubed
150ml/¼ pint/⅔ cup unsweetened soya milk

1 Put the dates in a pan. Pour in 300ml/½ pint/1¼ cups of the apple juice and leave to soak for 2 hours. Simmer for 10 minutes, then leave to cool. Using a slotted spoon, lift out one-quarter of the dates, chop roughly and set aside.

2 Purée the remaining dates in a food processor or blender. Add the cinnamon and process with enough of the remaining apple juice to make a smooth paste.

3 Add the cubes of tofu, a few at a time, processing after each addition. Finally, add the remaining apple juice and the soya milk.

4 Pour the mixture into a freezer container and freeze for 4 hours, beating twice to break up the ice crystals.

5 Alternatively, use an ice cream maker. Churn until thick, but not firm enough to scoop. Turn into a freezer container.

6 Stir in most of the chopped dates and freeze for 2–3 hours until firm. To serve, scoop the ice into dessert glasses and decorate with the remaining chopped dates.

> **Cook's Tip**
> As tofu is a non-dairy product, it will not blend completely, so don't be concerned if the mixture contains tiny flecks of tofu.

Fresh Fruit Salad

A refreshing and colourful fruit salad, packed with Vitamin C, makes a healthy finale for any occasion.

Serves 6
2 eating apples
2 oranges
2 peaches
16–20 strawberries
30ml/2 tbsp freshly squeezed lemon juice
15–30ml/1–2 tbsp orange flower water
icing (confectioners') sugar, to taste (optional)
a few sprigs of fresh mint, to decorate

1 Peel and core the apples and cut into thin slices. Cut a thin slice of peel and pith from both ends of the oranges, then cut off the remaining peel and pit. Cut out each segment, leaving the membranes behind. Squeeze the juice from the membranes; reserve the juice and discard the membranes.

2 Blanch the peaches for 1 minute in boiling water, then peel off the skin and cut the flesh into thick slices.

3 Hull the strawberries, if you like, and halve or quarter if large. Place all the fruit in a large serving bowl.

4 Blend together the lemon juice, orange flower water and any orange juice. Taste and add a little icing sugar to sweeten, if you like. Pour the fruit juice mixture over the salad and serve decorated with mint leaves.

> **Cook's Tips**
> • There are no rules with this fruit salad, and you could use almost any fruit that you like. Oranges, however, should form the base and apples give a delightful contrast in texture.
> • As far as healthy desserts go, a fruit salad is hard to beat. Low in calories, yet high in fibre and a good source of Vitamin C, fresh fruit is nutritionally important and serving it as a salad is an excellent way of including it in the diet.

Date & Tofu Ice Energy 290Kcal/1232kJ; Protein 9.1g; Carbohydrate 58.2g, of which sugars 57.9g; Fat 3.9g, of which saturates 0.5g; Cholesterol 0mg; Calcium 407mg; Fibre 2.5g; Sodium 24mg.
Fresh Fruit Salad Energy 39Kcal/167kJ; Protein 1g; Carbohydrate 9.1g, of which sugars 9.1g; Fat 0.1g, of which saturates 0g; Cholesterol 0mg; Calcium 27mg; Fibre 1.8g; Sodium 5mg.

Fresh Citrus Jelly

Shimmering fresh fruit jellies really are worth the effort – they're packed with fresh flavour, natural colour and vitamins, plus they make a lovely fat-free dessert.

Serves 4

3 medium oranges
1 lemon
1 lime
75g/3oz/scant ½ cup golden caster (superfine) sugar
300ml/½ pint/1¼ cups water
15ml/1 tbsp/1 sachet powdered gelatine
extra slices of fruit, to decorate

1 With a sharp knife, cut all the peel and white pith from one orange and carefully remove the segments from between the membranes. Arrange the segments in the base of a 900ml/1½ pint/3¾ cup mould or dish.

2 Pare off some citrus rind, cut into shreds and reserve them for decoration. Grate the remaining rind from the lemon and lime and one orange. Place all the grated rind in a pan, with the sugar and the water.

3 Heat gently until the sugar has dissolved, without boiling. Remove from the heat. Squeeze the juice from all the rest of the fruit and stir it into the pan.

4 Strain the liquid into a measuring jug (cup) to remove the rind (you should have about 600ml/1 pint/2½ cups: if necessary, make up the amount with water). Sprinkle the gelatine over the liquid and stir until it has completely dissolved.

5 Pour a little of the jelly over the orange segments and chill until set. Leave the remaining jelly at room temperature to cool, but do not allow it to set.

6 Pour the remaining cooled jelly into the dish and chill until set. To serve, turn out the jelly on to a serving plate and decorate it with the reserved citrus rind shreds and extra slices of citrus fruit.

Strawberries in Spiced Grape Jelly

A subtle touch of cinnamon is combined with juicy strawberries and orange juice to make a fresh-tasting dessert that is fat free and vitamin rich.

Serves 4

475ml/16fl oz/2 cups red grape juice
1 cinnamon stick
1 small orange
15ml/1 tbsp powdered gelatine
225g/8oz/2 cups strawberries, chopped, plus extra to decorate

1 Pour the grape juice into a pan and add the cinnamon stick. Thinly pare the rind from the orange. Add most of it to the pan but shred some pieces and set them aside for the decoration.

2 Place the pan over a very low heat for 10 minutes, then remove the flavourings from the grape juice.

3 Squeeze the juice from the orange into a bowl and sprinkle over the powdered gelatine. When the mixture is spongy, stir into the grape juice until it has completely dissolved. Allow the jelly to cool until just beginning to set.

4 Stir in the strawberries and quickly turn into a 1 litre/1¾ pint/4 cup mould or serving dish. Chill until set.

5 To serve, dip the mould quickly into hot water and turn the jelly out on to a serving plate. Decorate with strawberries and shreds of orange rind.

> **Cook's Tip**
> *Do not wash strawberries until just before you hull them. Quickly dip them in water, then pat dry on kitchen paper.*

> **Variation**
> *Fresh raspberries can be used instead of strawberries.*

Citrus Jelly Energy 107Kcal/458kJ; Protein 1.1g; Carbohydrate 27.3g, of which sugars 27.3g; Fat 0.1g, of which saturates 0g; Cholesterol 0mg; Calcium 52mg; Fibre 1.5g; Sodium 6mg.
Strawberries in Grape Jelly Energy 81Kcal/344kJ; Protein 1.1g; Carbohydrate 19.8g, of which sugars 19.8g; Fat 0.2g, of which saturates 0g; Cholesterol 0mg; Calcium 46mg; Fibre 1.1g; Sodium 13mg.

Orange-Blossom Jelly

A fresh orange jelly makes a delightful dessert; the natural fruit flavour combined with the smooth jelly has a wonderful cleansing quality.

Serves 4
65g/2½oz/5 tbsp caster (superfine) sugar
150ml/¼ pint/⅔ cup water
25g/1oz powdered gelatine
600ml/1 pint/2½ cups fresh orange juice
30ml/2 tbsp orange flower water
unsprayed edible flowers, to decorate (optional)

1 Place the caster sugar and water in a small pan and heat gently to dissolve the sugar. Pour into a heatproof bowl and leave to cool.

2 Sprinkle the gelatine over the surface of the syrup. Leave to stand until the gelatine has absorbed all the liquid.

3 Gently melt the gelatine over a pan of simmering water until it becomes clear and transparent. Leave to cool. When the gelatine mixture is cold, mix it with the orange juice and orange flower water.

4 Wet a jelly mould or bowl and pour in the jelly. Chill in the refrigerator for at least 2 hours, or until set.

5 To serve, dip the mould quickly into hot water and turn the jelly out on to a serving plate. Decorate the edge of the jelly with edible flowers, if you like.

Grapes in Grape-Yogurt Jelly

Grapes can do you a power of good and here they are combined with low-fat yogurt to make a stylish dessert for a dinner party.

Serves 4
250g/9oz/2¼ cups white seedless grapes
450ml/¾ pint/scant 2 cups unsweetened white grape juice
15ml/1 tbsp powdered gelatine
120ml/4fl oz/½ cup low-fat natural (plain) yogurt

1 Set aside four tiny bunches of grapes for decoration. Pull the rest off their stalks and cut them in half.

2 Divide the grapes among four stemmed glasses and tilt the glasses on one side, propping them firmly in a bowl of ice.

3 Place the grape juice in a pan and heat it until almost boiling. Remove it from the heat and sprinkle the gelatine over the surface, stirring to dissolve the gelatine.

4 Pour half the grape juice over the grapes and leave to set.

5 Cool the remaining grape juice until on the verge of setting, then stir in the low-fat natural yogurt.

6 Stand the set glasses upright and pour in the yogurt mixture. Chill to set, then decorate the rim of each glass with grapes, and serve.

> ### Cook's Tip
> *For an easier version, stand the glasses upright rather than at an angle – then they can be put in the refrigerator to set rather than packed with ice.*

> ### Variation
> *You could always use small red grapes instead of green.*

> ### Cook's Tips
> *• If you are entertaining, make this jelly extra-special by substituting Grand Marnier for the orange flower water.*
> *• For a vegetarian version, use an alternative gelling agent such as agar-agar, which is produced from seaweed. Treat as for gelatine but bear in mind that agar-agar has to boil to dissolve.*

Grapes in Jelly Energy 106Kcal/452kJ; Protein 2.1g; Carbohydrate 25.1g, of which sugars 25.1g; Fat 0.5g, of which saturates 0.2g; Cholesterol 0mg; Calcium 87mg; Fibre 0.5g; Sodium 34mg.
Orange-Blossom Jelly Energy 118Kcal/503kJ; Protein 0.8g; Carbohydrate 30.2g, of which sugars 30.2g; Fat 0.2g, of which saturates 0g; Cholesterol 0mg; Calcium 24mg; Fibre 0.2g; Sodium 16mg.

Mandarins in Orange Flower Syrup

Whole mandarins, bathed in a fragrant juice, create a healthy fruit dessert that's bursting with fresh flavours. A perfect, palate-tingling way to end any meal.

Serves 4
10 fresh mandarins
15ml/1 tbsp icing (confectioners') sugar
10ml/2 tsp orange flower water
15ml/1 tbsp unsalted pistachio nuts, shelled and chopped

1 Thinly pare a little of the rind from one mandarin with a vegetable peeler and cut it into fine shreds for decoration. Squeeze the juice from two of the mandarins and reserve.

2 Peel the remaining fruit, removing as much of the white pith as possible. Arrange the whole fruits in a wide dish.

3 Mix the reserved juice with the sugar and orange flower water, then pour over the fruit. Cover the dish and chill for at least 1 hour.

4 Blanch the shreds of rind in boiling water for 30 seconds. Drain and leave to cool.

5 Sprinkle the rind shreds and chopped pistachio nuts over the mandarins in the dish and serve.

Cook's Tips
• The mandarins look very attractive if you leave them whole, especially if there is a large quantity for a special occasion, but you may prefer to separate the segments.
• This dish is suitable for any of the other small-size citrus fruits. Tangerines, clementines, mineolas and satsumas would all work very well instead of mandarins.
• If you want to serve the dish with an accompaniment, try yogurt-based ice cream or low-fat crème fraîche to keep on a healthy note.

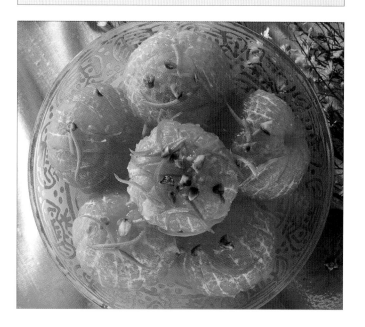

Chilled Oranges in Syrup

This popular classic is a refreshing way to serve up oranges, which are packed with Vitamin C and dietary fibre – vital for good health.

Serves 4
4 oranges
600ml/1 pint/2½ cups water
350g/12oz/1½ cups granulated sugar
30ml/2 tbsp freshly squeezed lemon juice
30ml/2 tbsp rose water
40g/1½oz/¼ cup unsalted pistachio nuts, shelled and chopped

1 Pare the rind from the oranges with a vegetable peeler, leaving the white pith on the fruit.

2 Cut the orange rind into fine strips and boil in water several times to remove the bitterness. Drain on kitchen paper.

3 Place the water, sugar and lemon juice in a pan. Bring to the boil, add the pared orange rind strips and simmer until the syrup thickens and turns to a syrup. Add the rose water, stir and leave to cool.

4 Peel away the pith from the oranges, then cut the fruit crossways into neat slices. Arrange in a serving dish and pour over the flavoured syrup.

5 Chill the oranges for 1–2 hours. Sprinkle with the pistachio nuts before serving.

Cook's Tips
• Almonds could be substituted for the pistachio nuts, if you like, but don't be tempted to increase the quantity or you'll raise the level of fat.
• If they are available, use blood red oranges to add an interesting colour to the dish.

Chilled Oranges Energy 449Kcal/1909kJ; Protein 3.6g; Carbohydrate 102.5g, of which sugars 102.2g; Fat 5.7g, of which saturates 0.8g; Cholesterol 0mg; Calcium 114mg; Fibre 2.7g; Sodium 64mg.
Mandarins in Syrup Energy 74Kcal/314kJ; Protein 1.6g; Carbohydrate 12.9g, of which sugars 12.8g; Fat 2.2g, of which saturates 0.3g; Cholesterol 0mg; Calcium 37mg; Fibre 1.4g; Sodium 24mg.

Crispy Mango Stacks with Raspberry Coulis

This makes an extremely healthy yet impressively attractive dessert – it is low in fat and also contains no added sugar. However, if the fresh raspberries prove to be a little sharp to the taste, then you may prefer to add a pinch of sugar to the fruit purée.

Serves 4

3 filo pastry sheets, thawed
    if frozen
2 small ripe mangoes
115g/4oz/²⁄₃ cup raspberries,
    thawed if frozen
45ml/3 tbsp water
50g/2oz/¹⁄₄ cup butter,
    melted

1 Preheat the oven to 200°C/400°F/Gas 6. Lay the filo sheets on a clean work surface and cut out four 10cm/4in rounds from each.

2 Brush each round with the melted butter and lay them out on two baking sheets.

3 Bake the filo rounds for 5 minutes, or until they are crisp and golden in colour. Place on wire racks to cool.

4 Peel the mangoes, then remove the stones (pits) and cut the flesh into thin slices. Put the fresh raspberries in a food processor along with the water and process until the mixture has formed a purée; press the raspberry purée through a sieve (strainer).

5 Place a filo pastry round on each of four individual plates. Top with a quarter of the mango and drizzle with a little of the raspberry purée.

6 Repeat layering in this way until all of the ingredients have been used, finishing off with a layer of mango and a drizzle of the raspberry purée.

7 Serve immediately; this dessert is best served straight away.

Strawberries with Cointreau

Strawberries and oranges make a brilliant partnership. This dish is a glamorous way to have a portion of your daily fruit intake.

Serves 4

1 unwaxed orange
40g/1¹⁄₂oz/3 tbsp granulated
    sugar

75ml/5 tbsp water
450g/1lb/3¹⁄₂ cups strawberries,
    hulled
45ml/3 tbsp Cointreau or other
    orange-flavoured liqueur
250ml/8fl oz/1 cup low-fat
    Greek (US strained plain)
    yogurt

1 With a vegetable peeler, remove wide strips of rind from the orange, taking care to avoid the pith. Stack two or three pieces at a time and cut into very thin strips.

2 Mix the sugar and water in a small pan. Heat gently, swirling the pan occasionally until the sugar has dissolved. Bring to the boil, add the orange rind strips, then simmer for 10 minutes. Remove the pan from the heat and set the syrup aside to cool completely.

3 Reserve four strawberries for decoration and cut the rest lengthways in halves or quarters. Put them in a bowl. Stir the Cointreau or chosen liqueur into the syrup and pour it over the fruit with the orange rind. Set aside for at least 30 minutes or for up to 2 hours.

4 Whip the yogurt briefly, then sweeten to taste with a little of the syrup from the strawberries.

5 Spoon the chopped strawberries into glass serving dishes and top with dollops of the sweetened Greek yogurt. Decorate with the reserved strawberries.

> **Variation**
> *Use a mixture of soft summer fruit to ring the changes.*

Mango Stacks Energy 194Kcal/815kJ; Protein 2.4g; Carbohydrate 23.6g, of which sugars 12g; Fat 10.7g, of which saturates 6.7g; Cholesterol 27mg; Calcium 40mg; Fibre 3.1g; Sodium 79mg.
Strawberries Energy 151Kcal/638kJ; Protein 4.5g; Carbohydrate 27.2g, of which sugars 27.2g; Fat 0.8g, of which saturates 0.3g; Cholesterol 1mg; Calcium 156mg; Fibre 1.8g; Sodium 62mg.

Cinnamon & Apricot Soufflés

Don't expect this to be difficult simply because it's a soufflé – it really couldn't be easier, and, best of all, it's relatively low in fat. The cinnamon gives the dish a subtle spicy flavour that makes you want to come back for more.

Serves 4

low-fat spread, for greasing
plain (all-purpose) flour,
   for dusting
3 eggs
115g/4oz/^{1}/$_2$ cup apricot fruit
   spread
finely grated rind of ^{1}/$_2$ lemon
5ml/1 tsp ground cinnamon, plus
   extra to decorate

1 Preheat the oven to 190°C/375°F/Gas 5. Lightly grease four individual soufflé dishes and dust them lightly with flour.

2 Separate the eggs and place the yolks in a bowl with the fruit spread, lemon rind and cinnamon.

3 Whisk hard until the mixture is thick and pale in colour.

4 Place the egg whites in a grease-free bowl and whisk them until they form soft peaks when the whisk is lifted.

5 Using a metal spoon or spatula, gradually fold the egg whites evenly into the yolk mixture.

6 Divide the soufflé mixture among the prepared dishes and bake for 10–15 minutes, until well risen and golden brown. Serve immediately, dusted with a little extra ground cinnamon.

> **Variations**
> • Other fruit spreads would be delicious in this soufflé. Try peach or blueberry for a change.
> • Puréed, well-drained canned fruit can be used instead of the apricot spread, but make sure that the mixture is not too wet or the soufflés will not rise properly. Puréed fresh soft fruit can also be used but may need to be cooked before being puréed.

Apricot Delight

A layered treat for those who are watching their fat intake.

Serves 4
two 400g/14oz cans apricots in
   natural juice
50ml/2fl oz/^{1}/$_4$ cup fructose

15ml/1 tbsp lemon juice
25ml/1^1/$_2$ tbsp powdered gelatine
425g/15 oz/1^3/$_4$ cups low-fat
   custard
150ml/^{1}/$_4$ cup/^{2}/$_3$ cup low-fat
   natural (plain) thick yogurt
sliced apricot, fresh mint and yogurt
   piping cream, to decorate

1 Line the bottom of a 1.2 litre/2 pint/5 cup heart-shaped or round cake tin (pan) with baking parchment.

2 Drain the apricots, reserving the juice. Put the drained apricots in a food processor or blender. Add the fructose and 50ml/2fl oz/^{1}/$_4$ cup of the apricot juice. Blend to a purée.

3 Measure 15ml/1 tbsp of the apricot juice into a small bowl. Add the lemon juice, then sprinkle 10ml/2 tsp of the gelatine over. Set aside for 5 minutes until softened.

4 Stir the gelatine into half the apricot purée and pour into the cake tin. Chill in the refrigerator for 1^1/$_2$ hours, or until firm.

5 Sprinkle the remaining gelatine over 50ml/2fl oz/^{1}/$_4$ cup of the apricot juice. Soak and dissolve as before. Mix the remaining apricot purée with the custard, yogurt and gelatine. Pour on to the layer of set fruit purée and chill for 3 hours.

6 Dip the cake tin in hot water for a few seconds and unmould the heart on to a serving plate. Decorate with piped yogurt cream (see Cook's Tip box), apricot and mint.

> **Cook's Tip**
> For yogurt piping cream, dissolve 10ml/2 tsp powdered gelatine in 45ml/3 tbsp water then mix with 300ml/^{1}/$_2$ pint/1^1/$_4$ cups thick yogurt, 15ml/1 tbsp fructose and 2.5ml/^{1}/$_2$ tsp vanilla extract, chill for 30 minutes, then fold in a beaten egg white. Use to pipe.

Cinn. & Apricot Soufflés Energy 143Kcal/604kJ; Protein 5.2g; Carbohydrate 22.8g, of which sugars 19.9g; Fat 4.2g, of which saturates 1.2g; Cholesterol 143mg; Calcium 30mg; Fibre 0.1g; Sodium 61mg.
Apricot Delight Energy 193Kcal/823kJ; Protein 5.8g; Carbohydrate 36.9g, of which sugars 33.2g; Fat 2.5g, of which saturates 0.2g; Cholesterol 3mg; Calcium 210mg; Fibre 1.9g; Sodium 85mg.

Souffléed Orange Semolina

If your opinion of semolina is coloured by the memory of sloppy school puddings, treat yourself to a taste of this delicious version. Healthy grains have never tasted better.

Serves 4
50g/2oz/⅓ cup semolina
600ml/1 pint/2½ cups semi-skimmed (low-fat) milk
25g/1oz/2 tbsp light muscovado (brown) sugar
1 large orange
1 egg white

1 Preheat the oven to 200°C/400°F/Gas 6. Put the semolina in a non-stick pan and add the milk and sugar. Stir over a moderate heat until the semolina is thickened and smooth. Remove from the heat.

2 Pare a few thin pieces of rind from the orange, shred and reserve for decoration. Finely grate the remaining rind. Cut all the peel and white pith from the orange and separate the flesh into equal segments, cutting between the membranes. Discard the membranes and stir the segments of flesh into the semolina, with the grated orange rind.

3 Whisk the egg white in a grease-free bowl until stiff but not dry, then fold lightly and evenly into the mixture. Spoon into a 1 litre/1¾ pint/4 cup ovenproof dish and bake in the oven for 15–20 minutes, until risen and golden brown. Sprinkle over the orange shreds and serve immediately.

> **Cook's Tip**
> *When using the rind of citrus fruit, scrub the fruit thoroughly before use, or buy unwaxed fruit.*

> **Variation**
> *For rosy-flecked semolina, use fresh raspberries in place of the orange segments and decorate with a few whole berries.*

Filo Chiffon Pie

Filo pastry is low in fat and is very easy to use. Keep a pack in the freezer, ready to make impressive desserts like this one.

Serves 3
500g/1¼lb pink rhubarb
5ml/1 tsp mixed spice (apple pie spice)
finely grated rind and juice of 1 orange
15ml/1 tbsp caster (superfine) sugar
15g/½oz/1 tbsp butter
3 sheets filo pastry

1 Preheat the oven to 200°C/400°F/Gas 6. Trim the leaves and ends from the rhubarb sticks and chop them in to 2.5cm/1in pieces. Place in a bowl.

2 Add the mixed spice, orange rind and juice and sugar and toss well to coat evenly. Transfer the rhubarb to a 1 litre/ 1¾ pint/4 cup pie dish.

3 Melt the butter and brush it over the pastry sheets. Lift the pastry sheets on to the pie dish, butter-side up, and crumple to form a chiffon effect, covering the pie completely.

4 Place the dish on a baking sheet and bake in the oven for 20 minutes, until golden brown. Reduce the heat to 180°C/350°F/ Gas 4 and bake for a further 10–15 minutes, until the rhubarb is tender. Serve warm.

> **Cook's Tip**
> *When buying rhubarb, choose young, slender, pink stems, as these will be the most tender.*

> **Variation**
> *Other fruit, such as apples, pears or peaches, can be used in this pie – try it with whatever is in season.*

Orange Semolina Energy 159Kcal/676kJ; Protein 7.6g; Carbohydrate 27.8g, of which sugars 18.1g; Fat 2.8g, of which saturates 1.6g; Cholesterol 9mg; Calcium 204mg; Fibre 0.9g; Sodium 84mg.
Filo Chiffon Pie Energy 109Kcal/461kJ; Protein 2.6g; Carbohydrate 15.8g, of which sugars 8.2g; Fat 4.4g, of which saturates 2.6g; Cholesterol 11mg; Calcium 174mg; Fibre 2.7g; Sodium 38mg.

Hot Blueberry & Pear Soufflés

Blueberries are deliciously fragrant, with a flavour that is simultaneously sharp and sweet. Combining them with the slightly acidic, yet creamy, richness of pears is truly inspired. Make sure that you choose a good culinary pear.

Serves 6

low-fat spread, for greasing
150g/5oz/¾ cup caster (superfine) sugar, plus extra for dusting
350g/12oz/3 cups blueberries
2 medium pears, peeled, cored and finely diced
grated rind and juice of 1 pink grapefruit
3 egg whites
icing (confectioners') sugar, for dusting

1 Preheat the oven to 200°C/400°F/Gas 6. Grease six 150ml/¼ pint/⅔ cup soufflé dishes and dust with caster sugar. Put a baking sheet in the oven to heat.

2 Cook the blueberries and pears with the grapefruit rind and juice in a pan for 10 minutes. Press through a sieve (strainer) into a bowl. Stir in 50g/2oz/¼ cup of the caster sugar. Set aside to cool.

3 Put a spoonful of the blueberry and pear purée into each prepared dish and smooth the surface. Reserve the remaining purée and set the dishes aside.

4 Whisk the egg whites in a large grease-free bowl until they form stiff peaks. Very gradually whisk in the remaining caster sugar to make a stiff, glossy meringue mixture. Fold in the remaining blueberry and pear purée and spoon the flavoured meringue into the prepared dishes. Level the tops with a palette knife, and run a table knife around the edge of each dish.

5 Place the filled dishes on the hot baking sheet and bake in the oven for 10–15 minutes until the soufflés have risen well and are lightly browned.

6 Dust the tops of the soufflés with icing sugar. Serve immediately.

Mango & Ginger Clouds

The sweet, perfumed flavour of ripe mango combines beautifully with ginger, and this low-fat dessert makes the very most of them both.

Serves 6

3 ripe mangoes
3 pieces preserved stem ginger, plus 45ml/3 tbsp syrup from the jar
75g/3oz/½ cup silken tofu
3 egg whites
6 unsalted pistachio nuts, chopped

1 Cut the mango flesh from the stone (pit), remove the peel and chop the flesh.

2 Put the mango flesh in a food processor and add the ginger, syrup and tofu. Process until smooth. Spoon into a bowl.

3 Whisk the egg whites in a grease-free bowl until they form soft peaks. Fold them lightly into the mango mixture.

4 Spoon the mango mixture into either wide dishes or glasses and chill well before serving, sprinkled with the chopped pistachio nuts.

Cook's Tips
• Tofu, which is made from soya beans, has a high protein content yet is low in fat. It looks rather like cheese and is useful for vegetarian cooking. Firm tofu can be cut into chunks, while silken tofu has a softer consistency and is good for sauces. Although tofu has little taste, it readily absorbs other flavours, so is quite versatile.

Variation
Use toasted flaked (sliced) almonds or hazelnuts instead of the pistachios, or omit and decorate with extra mango slices.

Blueberry & Pear Energy 126Kcal/535kJ; Protein 2.2g; Carbohydrate 30.8g, of which sugars 30.8g; Fat 0.1g, of which saturates 0g; Cholesterol 0mg; Calcium 39mg; Fibre 2g; Sodium 34mg.
Mango & Ginger Clouds Energy 95Kcal/404kJ; Protein 3.5g; Carbohydrate 16.8g, of which sugars 16.5g; Fat 2.1g, of which saturates 0.3g; Cholesterol 0mg; Calcium 78mg; Fibre 2.1g; Sodium 66mg.

Bread & Sultana Custard

An old favourite gets the low-fat treatment and proves how successful this can be.

Serves 4
15ml/1 tbsp low-fat spread, plus extra for greasing
3 thin slices of bread, crusts removed
475ml/16fl oz/2 cups skimmed milk
2.5ml/½ tsp mixed spice (apple pie spice)
40g/1½oz/3 tbsp demerara (raw) sugar
2 eggs, whisked
75g/3oz/½ cup sultanas (golden raisins)
freshly grated nutmeg
a little icing (confectioners') sugar, for dusting

1 Preheat the oven to 180°C/350°F/Gas 4 and lightly grease an ovenproof dish. Spread the bread with low-fat spread and cut it into small pieces.

2 Place a layer of bread in the prepared dish, then continue layering until all the bread is used up.

3 Whisk together the skimmed milk, mixed spice, demerara sugar and eggs in a large mixing bowl. Pour the mixture over the complete surface of the bread. Sprinkle over the sultanas and leave to stand for 30 minutes.

4 Grate a little nutmeg over the top and bake for 30–40 minutes until the custard is just set and golden.

5 Serve the dessert immediately, dusted with icing sugar.

Variations
• White bread is the traditional choice for this dessert, but for a healthier dessert, use wholemeal (whole-wheat) or mixed grain bread, as this would provide extra fibre.
• Mix the sultanas with other dried fruits, such as chopped apricots or dates.

Poppyseed Custard with Red Fruit

Poppyseeds add a nutty flavour to this creamy custard without increasing the amount of fat too much.

Serves 6
low-fat spread, for greasing
600ml/1 pint/2½ cups skimmed milk
2 eggs
15ml/1 tbsp caster (superfine) sugar
15ml/1 tbsp poppyseeds
115g/4oz/1 cup each of strawberries, raspberries and blackberries
15ml/1 tbsp soft light brown sugar
60ml/4 tbsp red grape juice

1 Preheat the oven to 150°C/300°F/Gas 2. Grease a soufflé dish very lightly with low-fat spread. Heat the milk until just below boiling point, but do not boil. Beat the eggs in a bowl with the caster sugar and poppyseeds until creamy.

2 Whisk the milk into the egg mixture until very well mixed. Stand the prepared soufflé dish in a shallow roasting pan, then pour in hot water from a kettle to come halfway up the sides of the dish.

3 Pour the custard into the soufflé dish and bake in the preheated oven for 50–60 minutes, until the custard is just set and golden on top.

4 While the custard is cooking, mix the fruit with the brown sugar and fruit juice. Chill until ready to serve with the custard.

Variations
• If you don't like poppyseeds, sprinkle the surface of the custard with freshly grated nutmeg or ground cinnamon instead.
• Vary the mixed fruit according to what is available. A combination of exotic fruits would also look and taste delicious with the custard – just mix with orange or tropical juice and leave out the sugar, if you like.
• Cook the custard in individual ovenproof dishes, if you wish.

Tofu Berry Brûlée

Brûlée desserts are usually totally out of bounds on a low-fat diet, but this version is perfectly acceptable because it uses tofu, which is both low in fat and free from cholesterol.

Serves 4
300g/11oz packet silken tofu
45g/1¾oz/3 tbsp icing (confectioners') sugar
225g/8oz/2 cups red berry fruits, such as raspberries, strawberries and redcurrants
about 65g/2½oz/5 tbsp demerara (raw) sugar

1 Mix the tofu and the icing sugar in a food processor or a blender and process until smooth.

2 Stir in the fruits, then spoon the tofu and fruit mixture into a 900ml/1½ pint/3¾ cup flameproof dish. Flatten the top.

3 Sprinkle the top with enough demerara sugar to cover evenly. Place under a very hot grill (broiler) until the sugar melts and caramelizes. Chill before serving.

Cook's Tip
You should choose silken tofu as firm tofu does not have a smooth enough texture for this kind of dish.

Variation/Passion Fruit Brûlées
Cut 4 passion fruit in half with a sharp knife. Use a teaspoon to scoop out the pulp and seeds; divide among 4 ovenproof ramekins. Spoon equal amounts of 300ml/½ pint/1¼ cups low-fat Greek (US strained plain) yogurt on top of the fruit and smooth the surface level. Chill for at least 2 hours. Put 75g/3oz /6 tbsp soft light brown sugar in a small pan with 15ml/1 tbsp water and heat gently, stirring, until the sugar has melted and caramelized. Pour over the yogurt; the caramel will harden within 1 minute. Keep the brûlées in a cool place until ready to serve.

Orange Yogurt Brûlées

Luxurious treats, much lower in fat than classic brûlées, which are made with cream, eggs and lots of sugar. Proof that low-fat desserts can still be creamy and delicious.

Serves 4
2 oranges
150ml/¼ pint/⅔ cup low-fat Greek (US strained plain) yogurt
60ml/4 tbsp half-fat crème fraîche
40g/1½oz/3 tbsp golden caster (superfine) sugar
25g/1oz/2 tbsp light muscovado (brown) sugar

1 With a sharp knife, cut away all the peel and white pith from the oranges and chop the fruit. Alternatively, cut the oranges into segments, cutting the flesh away from the membranes.

2 Place the fruit in the bottom of four individual flameproof dishes. Mix together the yogurt and crème fraîche and spoon the mixture over the oranges.

3 Mix together the two sugars and sprinkle them evenly over the tops of the dishes.

4 Place the dishes under a preheated, very hot grill (broiler) for 3–4 minutes or until the sugar melts and turns to a rich golden brown. Serve warm or cold.

Cook's Tip
You can now buy little gas blow torches for use in the kitchen. They make quick work of caramelizing the sugar on top of the brûlées — and are also fun to use!

Variation
Try replacing the oranges with peaches or raspberries.

Orange Yogurt Energy 91Kcal/385kJ; Protein 2.9g; Carbohydrate 16.3g, of which sugars 16.1g; Fat 2.1g, of which saturates 1.3g; Cholesterol 1mg; Calcium 114mg; Fibre 1g; Sodium 39mg.
Tofu Berry Brûlée Energy 187Kcal/794kJ; Protein 7g; Carbohydrate 34.5g, of which sugars 34.2g; Fat 3.3g, of which saturates 0.4g; Cholesterol 0mg; Calcium 413mg; Fibre 1.4g; Sodium 7mg.

Raspberry Passion Fruit Swirls

Quick and nutritious, this attractive fruit and yogurt dessert is the ideal choice for mid-week entertaining when you haven't got much time on your hands.

Serves 4

350g/12oz/2 cups raspberries
2 passion fruit
400ml/14fl oz/1⅔ cups low-fat fromage frais or Greek (US strained plain) yogurt
25g/1oz/2 tbsp caster (superfine) sugar
raspberries and fresh mint sprigs, to decorate

1 Using a fork, mash the raspberries in a small bowl until the juice runs.

2 Place the fromage frais and sugar in a separate bowl. Halve the passion fruit and scoop out the seeds. Add to the fromage frais and mix well.

3 Place alternate spoonfuls of the raspberry pulp and the fromage frais mixture into stemmed glasses or serving dishes.

4 Stir lightly to create a swirled effect. Decorate each dessert with a whole raspberry and a sprig of fresh mint. Serve chilled.

Cook's Tip
Use frozen raspberries when fresh are not available, but thaw them first. If passion fruit isn't available, flavour the yogurt mixture with finely grated orange rind instead.

Variations
This is a good recipe for using over-ripe, slightly soft fruit. The raspberries can be replaced by any summer fruit very successfully. Add chopped nuts or crumbled amaretti for added texture, but watch the fat content.

Strawberry Rose Petal Pashka

This lighter version of a traditional Russian dessert is ideal for dinner parties. The rose decoration is worth trying to do as it makes the dish look extremely pretty.

Serves 4

350g/12oz/1½ cups low-fat cottage cheese
175ml/6fl oz/¾ cup low-fat natural (plain) yogurt
30ml/2 tbsp clear honey
2.5ml/½ tsp rose water
275g/10oz/2½ cups strawberries
handful of scented pink rose petals, to decorate

1 Drain any free liquid from the cottage cheese and turn the cheese into a sieve (strainer). Rub it through the sieve into a bowl. Stir the yogurt, honey and rose water into the cheese.

2 Roughly chop about half the strawberries and fold them into the cheese mixture.

3 Line a new, clean flowerpot or a sieve (strainer) with fine muslin (cheesecloth) and add the cheese mixture. Leave the mixture to drain over a bowl for several hours or overnight.

4 Invert the flowerpot or sieve on to a serving plate, turn out the pashka and lift off the muslin. Cut the remaining strawberries in half and arrange them around the pashka. Scatter the rose petals over the top. Serve chilled.

Cook's Tip
Allow yourself enough time to make this dessert – for the best results, it needs to be drained overnight, then chilled well.

Variation
Use small porcelain heart-shaped moulds with draining holes for a pretty alternative.

Fruit Swirls Energy 109Kcal/466kJ; Protein 9g; Carbohydrate 18.5g, of which sugars 18.5g; Fat 0.5g, of which saturates 0.2g; Cholesterol 1mg; Calcium 111mg; Fibre 2.1g; Sodium 37mg.
Pashka Energy 153Kcal/643kJ; Protein 13.8g; Carbohydrate 15.9g, of which sugars 15.9g; Fat 3.9g, of which saturates 2.3g; Cholesterol 15mg; Calcium 206mg; Fibre 0.8g; Sodium 304mg.

Lemon Hearts with Strawberry Sauce

These elegant little hearts are perfect for a romantic celebration, such as a Valentine's Day dinner.

Serves 6

low-fat spread, for greasing
175g/6oz/¾ cup low-fat cottage cheese
150ml/¼ pint/⅔ cup half-fat crème fraîche

15ml/1 tbsp granulated sugar
finely grated rind of ½ lemon
30ml/2 tbsp lemon juice
10ml/2 tsp powdered gelatine
2 egg whites

For the sauce

225g/8oz/2 cups fresh or frozen and thawed strawberries, plus extra to decorate
15ml/1 tbsp lemon juice

1 Lightly grease six individual heart-shaped moulds. Press the cottage cheese through a sieve (strainer) into a bowl. Beat in the crème fraîche, sugar and lemon rind.

2 Pour the lemon juice into a small heatproof bowl and sprinkle the gelatine over the surface. When it has soaked in, place the bowl over a pan of hot water and stir to dissolve the gelatine completely.

3 Quickly stir the gelatine into the cheese mixture, making sure that it is mixed in evenly.

4 Beat the egg whites in a grease-free bowl until they form soft peaks. Quickly fold them into the cheese mixture.

5 Carefully spoon the mixture into the six prepared moulds, and chill until set.

6 Make the sauce. Mix the strawberries and lemon juice in a food processor or blender and process until smooth.

7 Pour the sauce on to serving plates and then carefully invert the lemon hearts to lie on top of the sauce. Decorate with slices of strawberry.

Rice Pudding with Mixed Berry Sauce

In this recipe, a compote of red berries contrasts brilliantly with creamy rice pudding to create a delicious yet nutritionally well-balanced dessert.

Serves 6

low-fat spread, for greasing
400g/14oz/2 cups pudding (short-grain) rice
325ml/11fl oz/scant 1½ cups skimmed milk
pinch salt
115g/4oz/scant ½ cup soft light brown sugar

5ml/1 tsp vanilla extract
2 eggs, beaten
grated rind of 1 lemon
5ml/1 tsp lemon juice
30ml/2 tbsp low-fat spread
strawberry leaves, to decorate

For the sauce

225g/8oz/2 cups strawberries, hulled and quartered
225g/8oz/1⅓ cups raspberries
115g/4oz/½ cup granulated sugar
grated rind of 1 lemon

1 Preheat the oven to 160°C/325°F/Gas 3. Grease a deep 2 litre/3½ pint/8 cup baking dish. Add the rice to a pan of boiling water and boil for 5 minutes. Drain. Transfer the rice to the prepared baking dish.

2 Combine the milk, salt, brown sugar, vanilla extract, eggs, and lemon rind and juice. Pour over the rice and stir.

3 Dot the surface of the rice mixture with the spread. Bake for about 50 minutes until the rice is cooked and creamy.

4 Meanwhile, make the sauce. Mix the berries and sugar in a small pan. Stir over low heat until the sugar dissolves completely and the fruit is becoming pulpy. Transfer to a bowl and stir in the lemon rind. Cool, then chill until required.

5 Remove the rice pudding from the oven and allow to cool. Serve with the berry sauce and decorate each serving with strawberry leaves.

Lemon Hearts Energy 90Kcal/376kJ; Protein 4.7g; Carbohydrate 6.9g, of which sugars 6.5g; Fat 4.9g, of which saturates 3.2g; Cholesterol 5mg; Calcium 68mg; Fibre 0.4g; Sodium 99mg.
Rice Pudding Energy 461Kcal/1942kJ; Protein 9.7g; Carbohydrate 100.2g, of which sugars 47g; Fat 3.4g, of which saturates 0.8g; Cholesterol 66mg; Calcium 121mg; Fibre 0.8g; Sodium 63mg.

Strawberry & Apple Crumble

A high-fibre, low-fat version of the classic apple crumble that will appeal to both children and adults alike.

2.5ml/½ tsp ground cinnamon
30ml/2 tbsp orange juice
low-fat custard or yogurt, to serve
(optional)

Serves 4
450g/1lb cooking apples
150g/5oz/1¼ cups strawberries, hulled
25g/1oz/2 tbsp caster (superfine) sugar

For the crumble
45g/1¾oz/3 tbsp plain (all-purpose) wholemeal (whole-wheat) flour
50g/2oz/⅔ cup rolled oats
30ml/2 tbsp low-fat spread

1 Preheat the oven to 180°C/350°F/Gas 4. Peel, core and cut the apples into approximately 5mm/¼in size slices. Halve the strawberries.

2 Toss together the apples, strawberries, sugar, cinnamon and orange juice. Transfer the mixture to a 1.2 litre/2 pint/5 cup ovenproof dish.

3 Make the crumble. Combine the flour and oats in a bowl and mix in the low-fat spread with a fork.

4 Sprinkle the crumble evenly over the fruit. Bake for 40–45 minutes, until golden brown and bubbling. Serve warm, with low-fat custard or yogurt, if you like.

> **Cook's Tip**
> Strawberries and apples are a good source of Vitamin C, which plays an important role in a healthy diet.

> **Variations**
> Blackberries, raspberries or redcurrants can be used instead of the strawberries very successfully.

Chunky Apple Bake

An apple a day keeps the doctor away, as they say. Apples are certainly a good source of Vitamin C and fibre, so this wholesome dish is full of goodness.

Serves 4
450g/1lb cooking apples
75g/3oz wholemeal (whole-wheat) bread, crusts removed
115g/4oz/½ cup low-fat cottage cheese
40g/1½oz/3 tbsp light muscovado (brown) sugar
200ml/7fl oz/scant 1 cup skimmed milk
5ml/1 tsp demerara (raw) sugar

1 Preheat the oven to 220°C/425°F/Gas 7. Peel the apples, cut them into quarters and remove the cores.

2 Using a sharp knife, roughly chop the apples into even-size pieces, about 1cm/½in in width and depth.

3 Cut the bread into 1cm/½in cubes. Do not use crusts as these will be too thick for the mixture.

4 Put the apples in a bowl and add the bread cubes, cottage cheese and muscovado sugar. Toss lightly to mix.

5 Stir in the skimmed milk and then turn the mixture into a wide ovenproof dish. Sprinkle demerara sugar over the top of the mixture.

6 Bake for 30–35 minutes, or until the apple bake is golden brown and bubbling. Serve hot.

> **Cook's Tip**
> You may need to adjust the amount of milk used, depending on the dryness of the bread; the staler it is, the more milk it will absorb. The texture should be very moist but not falling apart.

Strawb. & Apple Crumble Energy 200Kcal/846kJ; Protein 3.8g; Carbohydrate 38.7g, of which sugars 21g; Fat 4.4g, of which saturates 0.9g; Cholesterol 0mg; Calcium 41mg; Fibre 3.4g; Sodium 59mg.
Apple Bake Energy 170Kcal/721kJ; Protein 7.4g; Carbohydrate 32.7g, of which sugars 25.2g; Fat 1.9g, of which saturates 0.7g; Cholesterol 6mg; Calcium 120mg; Fibre 2.9g; Sodium 213mg.

Kumquat Compote

Warm, spicy and full of sun-ripened ingredients, this is the perfect winter dessert to remind you of long summer days – and to keep you in good shape.

Serves 4
200g/7oz/2 cups kumquats
200g/7oz/scant 1 cup ready-to-eat dried apricots
30ml/2 tbsp sultanas (golden raisins)

400ml/14fl oz/1⅔ cups water
1 orange
2.5cm/1in piece of fresh root ginger
4 cardamom pods
4 cloves
30ml/2 tbsp clear honey
15ml/1 tbsp flaked (sliced) almonds, toasted

1 Wash the kumquats, and, if they are large, cut them in half. Place them in a pan with the dried apricots, sultanas and water. Bring to the boil.

2 Pare the orange rind and add to the pan. Peel and grate the ginger and add to the pan. Crush the cardamom pods and add the seeds to the mixture, with the cloves.

3 Reduce the heat, cover the pan and leave to simmer gently for about 30 minutes, or until the kumquats are tender, stirring occasionally during cooking.

4 Squeeze the juice of the orange into the compote. Sweeten with the honey, sprinkle with the almonds and serve warm.

Cook's Tips
• Kumquats, which look like tiny oranges, can be eaten whole as their skins are thin and sweet tasting. They provide a delicious, distinctive citrus flavour to sweet and savoury dishes. Their season is short – if they are unavailable, use orange segments or sliced, peeled clementines instead.
• Try a full-flavoured honey made from clover, acacia or thyme.

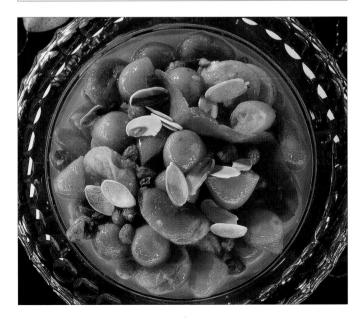

Baked Fruit Compote

This marvellous medley of dried fruit is the ultimate high-fibre dessert and is filled with natural sweetness.

Serves 6
115g/4oz/⅔ cup ready-to-eat dried figs
115g/4oz/½ cup ready-to-eat dried apricots
50g/2oz/½ cup ready-to-eat dried apple rings
50g/2oz/¼ cup ready-to-eat prunes

50g/2oz/½ cup ready-to-eat dried pears
50g/2oz/½ cup ready-to-eat dried peaches
300ml/½ pint/1¼ cups unsweetened apple juice
300ml/½ pint/1¼ cups unsweetened orange juice
6 cloves
1 cinnamon stick
a few toasted flaked (sliced) almonds, to decorate

1 Preheat the oven to 180°C/350°F/Gas 4. Place the figs, apricots, apple rings, prunes, pears and peaches in a shallow ovenproof dish and stir to mix.

2 Mix together the unsweetened apple and orange juices and pour evenly over the fruit. Add the cloves and cinnamon stick and stir gently to mix. Make sure that all the fruit has been thoroughly coated with the apple and orange juices.

3 Bake for about 30 minutes until the fruit mixture is hot, stirring once or twice during cooking. Set aside and leave to soak for 20 minutes. Discard the cloves and cinnamon stick.

4 Spoon the compote into serving bowls and serve warm or cold, decorated with toasted flaked almonds.

Fresh Figs with Honey & Wine

Fresh figs are naturally sweet, and they taste wonderful in a honeyed wine syrup.

Serves 6
450ml/¾ pint/scant 2 cups dry white wine
75g/3oz/⅓ cup clear honey
50g/2oz/¼ cup caster (superfine) sugar

1 small orange
8 whole cloves
450g/1lb fresh figs
1 cinnamon stick
bay leaves, to decorate

For the sauce
300ml/½ pint/1¼ cups low-fat Greek (US strained plain) yogurt
5ml/1 tsp pure vanilla extract
5ml/1 tsp caster (superfine) sugar

1 Put the wine, honey and sugar in a heavy pan and heat gently until the sugar dissolves.

2 Stud the orange with the cloves and add to the syrup with the figs and cinnamon. Cover and simmer until the figs are soft. Transfer to a serving dish and cool.

3 Flavour the yogurt with the vanilla and sugar and spoon into a serving dish. With a sharp knife, cut one or two of the figs in half, if you like, to show off their pretty centres. Decorate with the bay leaves and serve with the yogurt.

Kumquat Energy 348Kcal/1482kJ; Protein 5.3g; Carbohydrate 80.7g, of which sugars 80.6g; Fat 2.8g, of which saturates 0.2g; Cholesterol 0mg; Calcium 110mg; Fibre 5.5g; Sodium 25mg.
Baked Fruit Energy 160Kcal/683kJ; Protein 3g; Carbohydrate 37.8g, of which sugars 37.8g; Fat 0.7g, of which saturates 0g; Cholesterol 0mg; Calcium 91mg; Fibre 4.7g; Sodium 24mg.
Fresh Figs Energy 225Kcal/954kJ; Protein 3.9g; Carbohydrate 41g, of which sugars 41g; Fat 1g, of which saturates 0.3g; Cholesterol 1mg; Calcium 191mg; Fibre 2.5g; Sodium 67mg.

Plum, Apple & Banana Scone Pie

A simple, satisfying dish, the scrumptious topping hides a delicious mix of fruits.

Serves 4
450g/1lb plums
1 cooking apple
1 large banana
150ml/¼ cup/⅔ cup water

115g/4oz/1 cup wholemeal
  (whole-wheat) flour
10ml/2 tsp baking powder
45ml/3 tbsp raisins
50ml/2fl oz/¼ cup soured milk or
  low-fat natural (plain) yogurt
low-fat natural yogurt, to serve
  (optional)

1 Preheat the oven to 180°C/350°F/Gas 4. Cut the plums in half and ease out the stones (pits). Peel, core and chop the apple, then slice the banana.

2 Mix together all of the cut-up fruit in a pan. Pour in the water. Bring the mixture to simmering point and cook gently for about 15 minutes, or until all of the fruit is completely soft.

3 Spoon the cooked fruit mixture into a pie dish. Level the top.

4 Mix the flour, baking powder and raisins in a bowl. Add the soured milk or yogurt and mix to make a very soft dough.

5 Transfer the scone dough to a lightly floured surface and divide it up into 6–8 portions. Pat the dough portions into flattish scones.

6 Cover the plum and apple mixture with the scones. Bake the pie for about 40 minutes, or until the scone topping is completely cooked through. Serve with yogurt, if you like.

Almond Tart

This lower-fat version of a favourite tart is easy to make and bursts with nutty flavour.

Serves 4
225g/8oz puff pastry
30ml/2 tbsp raspberry or apricot
  jam

2 eggs
2 egg yolks
generous 50g/2oz/¼ cup caster
  (superfine) sugar
115g/4oz/½ cup butter, melted
50g/2oz/½ cup ground almonds
few drops of almond extract
icing (confectioners') sugar, for
  sifting

1 Preheat the oven to 200°C/400°F/Gas 6. Roll out the pastry on a lightly floured surface and use it to line an 18cm/7in pie plate or loose-bottomed flan tin (tart pan). Spread the jam over the bottom of the pastry case.

2 Whisk the eggs, egg yolks and sugar together in a large bowl until thick and pale. Gently stir the butter, ground almonds and almond extract into the mixture.

3 Pour the mixture into the pastry case and bake for about 30 minutes, until the filling is just set and browned. Sift icing sugar over the top before serving the tart hot, warm or cold.

Apple Brown Betty

A traditional favourite, this tasty dish is made up of delicious layers of lightly spiced toasted breadcrumbs and apples. It is very warming and satisfying, yet at the same time low in fat. Delicious served with fat-free yogurt.

Serves 6
50g/2oz/¾ cup fresh breadcrumbs
low-fat spread, for greasing
175g/6oz/1 cup light muscovado
  (brown) sugar
2.5ml/½ tsp ground cinnamon
1.5ml/¼ tsp ground cloves
1.5ml/¼ tsp grated nutmeg
900g/2lb eating apples
juice of 1 lemon
30ml/2 tbsp low-fat spread
20g/¾oz/3 tbsp finely chopped
  walnuts

1 Preheat the grill (broiler). Spread the breadcrumbs on a baking sheet and toast under the grill until golden, stirring so that they colour evenly. Set aside.

2 Preheat the oven to 190°C/375°F/Gas 5. Grease a 2 litre/3½ pint/8 cup baking dish.

3 Place the sugar in a medium-size mixing bowl and add the ground cinnamon, cloves and grated nutmeg. Mix well together.

4 Peel, core and slice the apples. Toss the apple slices with the lemon juice to prevent them from turning brown.

5 Sprinkle about 45ml/3 tbsp of the breadcrumbs over the bottom of the prepared dish. Cover with one-third of the apples and sprinkle one-third of the sugar-spice mixture on top.

6 Add another layer of breadcrumbs and dot with one-quarter of the spread. Repeat the layers two more times, ending with a layer of breadcrumbs. Sprinkle with the nuts, and dot with the remaining spread.

7 Bake for 35–40 minutes, until the apples are tender and the top is golden brown. Serve warm.

Scone Pie Energy 211Kcal/895kJ; Protein 5.2g; Carbohydrate 42.7g, of which sugars 24.5g; Fat 3.4g, of which saturates 1.7g; Cholesterol 8mg; Calcium 44mg; Fibre 5.1g; Sodium 16mg.
Almond Tart Energy 577Kcal/2394kJ; Protein 10.6g; Carbohydrate 24.4g, of which sugars 4g; Fat 49.9g, of which saturates 17.1g; Cholesterol 257mg; Calcium 94mg; Fibre 0.9g; Sodium 391mg.
Apple Brown Betty Energy 232Kcal/987kJ; Protein 2.3g; Carbohydrate 48.5g, of which sugars 42.3g; Fat 4.6g, of which saturates 0.8g; Cholesterol 0mg; Calcium 36mg; Fibre 2.7g; Sodium 101mg.

Blueberry Buckle

This wholesome dessert is an American speciality. A great way to turn vitamin-rich, juicy blueberries into a hearty family dessert.

Serves 8
low-fat spread, for greasing
225g/8oz/2 cups plain
   (all-purpose) flour
10ml/2 tsp baking powder
2.5ml/½ tsp salt
30ml/2 tbsp low-fat spread
175g/6oz/¾ cup caster
   (superfine) sugar
1 egg
2.5ml/½ tsp vanilla extract

175ml/6fl oz/¾ cup skimmed
   milk
450g/1lb/4 cups fresh blueberries
low-fat Greek (US strained plain)
   yogurt, to serve (optional)

For the topping
115g/4oz/scant ½ cup soft light
   brown sugar
50g/2oz/½ cup plain
   (all-purpose) flour
2.5ml/½ tsp salt
2.5ml/½ tsp ground allspice
45ml/3 tbsp low-fat spread
10ml/2 tsp skimmed milk
5ml/1 tsp pure vanilla extract

1 Preheat the oven to 190°C/375°F/Gas 5. Grease a 23cm/9in round gratin dish or shallow baking dish. Sift the flour, baking powder and salt into a bowl. Set aside.

2 Cream the low-fat spread and the sugar. Beat in the egg and vanilla extract. Add the flour mixture alternately with the milk, beginning and ending with flour.

3 Pour the mixture into the prepared dish and sprinkle over the blueberries.

4 Make the topping. Mix the brown sugar, flour, salt and allspice in a bowl. Rub in the spread with your fingertips until the mixture resembles coarse breadcrumbs.

5 Mix the milk and vanilla extract together. Drizzle over the flour mixture and mix with a fork. Sprinkle the topping over the blueberries. Bake for 45 minutes, or until a skewer inserted in the centre comes out clean. Serve warm, with low-fat Greek yogurt, if you like.

Cornflake-Topped Peach Bake

With just a few basic storecupboard ingredients, this healthy, crisp-crusted dish can be rustled up in next to no time. Just the job for an instant family meal.

Serves 4
415g/14½oz can peach slices
   in juice
30ml/2 tbsp sultanas (golden
   raisins)
1 cinnamon stick
strip of pared orange rind
30ml/2 tbsp low-fat spread
50g/2oz/1½ cups cornflakes
10ml/2 tsp sesame seeds

1 Preheat the oven to 200°C/400°F/Gas 6. Drain the peaches, reserving the juice in a small pan. Arrange the peach slices in a shallow ovenproof dish.

2 Add the sultanas, cinnamon stick and orange rind to the juice and bring to the boil. Lower the heat and simmer, for 3–4 minutes, to reduce the liquid by half. Remove the cinnamon stick and rind and spoon the syrup over the peaches.

3 Melt the low-fat spread in a small pan, stir in the cornflakes and sesame seeds.

4 Spread the cornflake mixture over the fruit. Bake for 15–20 minutes, or until the topping is crisp and golden. Serve hot.

Variations
• *Try experimenting with the breakfast cereal for the topping – the lowest-calorie breakfast cereals are usually those that are highest in fibre, so it is worth checking the labels for comparisons. Bran cereals are a good choice.*
• *You could use chopped nuts instead of the sesame seeds, but remember that this will increase the fat content.*
• *Any canned fruit can be used in place of the peaches. Apricots would be delicious, as would pineapple chunks. Make sure they are in their own natural juice.*

Blueberry Buckle Energy 329Kcal/1396kJ; Protein 6.4g; Carbohydrate 73.8g, of which sugars 42.4g; Fat 2.9g, of which saturates 0.7g; Cholesterol 25mg; Calcium 133mg; Fibre 3g; Sodium 48mg.
Peach Bake Energy 152Kcal/641kJ; Protein 2.7g; Carbohydrate 26.5g, of which sugars 16.4g; Fat 4.6g, of which saturates 1.1g; Cholesterol 0mg; Calcium 29mg; Fibre 1.3g; Sodium 188mg.

Barbecued Bananas with Spicy Vanilla Spread

Baked bananas are a must for the barbecue. As they are baked in their own skins, they create a fat-free dessert, and need no preparation at all. The vanilla and brandy spread adds a touch of luxury to the dish.

Serves 4
4 bananas
6 green cardamom pods
1 vanilla pod (bean)
finely grated rind of 1 small orange
30ml/2 tbsp brandy
50g/2oz/¼ cup light muscovado (brown) sugar
40g/1½oz/3 tbsp cup low-fat spread

1 Place the bananas, in their skins, on the hot barbecue and leave for 6–8 minutes, turning occasionally, until the skins are a brownish-black.

2 Meanwhile, split the cardamom pods and remove the seeds. Place the seeds in a mortar and crush lightly with a pestle.

3 Split the vanilla pod lengthways and scrape out the tiny seeds. Mix with the cardamom seeds, orange rind, brandy, sugar and spread, to make a thick paste.

4 Using a sharp knife, slit the skin of each banana and gently open out slightly. Spoon a little of the paste along each banana and serve immediately.

Cook's Tips
• *If making this for children, use orange juice instead of the brandy or, if the fat content is no object, drizzle the cooked bananas with melted chocolate.*
• *Bananas are a particularly nutritious fruit as they are rich in vitamins and minerals and have a good fibre content. Available throughout the year, they provide a healthy addition to the diet.*

Hot Spiced Bananas

Baking bananas in a rum and fruit syrup makes for a dessert with negligible fat and maximum flavour. Very easy to prepare, this dish is a delicious dish for impromptu entertaining.

Serves 6
low-fat spread, for greasing
6 ripe bananas
200g/7oz/1 cup light muscovado (brown) sugar
250ml/8fl oz/1 cup unsweetened pineapple juice
120ml/4fl oz/½ cup dark rum
2 cinnamon sticks
12 whole cloves

1 Preheat the oven to 180°C/350°F/Gas 4. Using low-fat spread, grease a 23cm/9in baking dish.

2 Peel the bananas and cut them diagonally into 2.5cm/1in pieces. Arrange the banana pieces evenly over the bottom of the prepared baking dish.

3 Mix the sugar and pineapple juice in a pan. Heat gently until the sugar has dissolved, stirring occasionally. Add the rum, cinnamon sticks and cloves. Bring to the boil, then remove the pan from the heat.

4 Pour the hot pineapple and spice mixture over the bananas in the baking dish. Bake in the preheated oven for about 25–30 minutes until the bananas are hot and very tender.

5 Divide the hot bananas between individual dishes, arranging them in a neat pattern. Serve immediately.

Cook's Tip
For an accompaniment that won't add too much to the fat content of this dessert, make your own frozen yogurt by churning an extra low-fat yogurt in an ice-cream maker until it has thickened. Serve a scoop with each serving.

Barbecued Bananas Energy 215Kcal/905kJ; Protein 1.9g; Carbohydrate 38.9g, of which sugars 36.6g; Fat 4.9g, of which saturates 1.4g; Cholesterol 1mg; Calcium 18mg; Fibre 1.1g; Sodium 75mg.
Spiced Bananas Energy 288Kcal/1221kJ; Protein 1.5g; Carbohydrate 62.4g, of which sugars 60.1g; Fat 0.3g, of which saturates 0.1g; Cholesterol 0mg; Calcium 27mg; Fibre 1.1g; Sodium 6mg.

Caribbean Bananas

Tender baked bananas for a
a feel-good dessert.

Serves 4
30ml/2 tbsp low-fat spread
8 firm ripe bananas
juice of 1 lime
75g/3oz/6 tbsp soft dark brown
  sugar

5ml/1 tsp ground allspice
2.5ml/½ tsp ground ginger
  seeds from 6 cardamoms, crushed
30ml/2 tbsp rum
pared lime rind, to decorate
half-fat crème fraîche, to serve
  (optional)

1 Preheat the oven to 200°C/400°F/Gas 6. Use a little of the spread to grease a shallow baking dish large enough to hold the bananas snugly in a single layer.

2 Peel the bananas and cut them in half lengthways. Arrange the bananas in the dish and pour over the lime juice.

3 Mix the sugar, allspice, ginger and crushed cardamom seeds in a bowl. Scatter the mixture over the bananas. Dot with the remaining low-fat spread. Bake, basting once, for 15 minutes, or until the bananas are soft.

4 Remove the dish from the oven. Warm the rum in a small pan or metal ladle, pour it over the bananas and set it alight.

5 As soon as the flames die down, decorate the dessert with the pared lime rind. Serve while still hot and add a dollop of low-fat crème fraîche to each portion, if you like.

Mulled Pears with Ginger & Brandy

Whole pears flavoured with spices and brandy – hard to beat as a simple yet elegant low-fat fruit dessert.

Serves 8
600ml/1 pint/2½ cups red wine
200g/7oz/1 cup sugar
1 cinnamon stick

6 cloves
finely grated rind of 1 orange
5ml/2 tsp grated fresh root ginger
8 even-size firm pears, with stems
15ml/1 tbsp brandy
25g/1oz/¼ cup almonds or
  hazelnuts, toasted, to decorate
low-fat whipped cream, to serve
  (optional)

1 Put all the ingredients except the pears, brandy and nuts into a pan large enough to hold the pears and heat slowly until the sugar has dissolved. Simmer for 5 minutes.

2 Peel the pears, leaving the stems on, and arrange upright in the pan. Cover and simmer for 45–50 minutes until tender.

3 Gently remove the pears from the syrup with a slotted spoon, being very careful not to dislodge the stems. Put the cooked pears in a serving bowl or individual bowls.

4 Boil the syrup until it thickens and reduces. Cool slightly, add the brandy and strain over the pears. Decorate with toasted nuts. Serve with whipped cream, if you like.

Floating Islands in Hot Plum Sauce

A low-fat version of the French classic that is simpler to make than it looks. The plum sauce can be made in advance, and reheated just before you cook the meringues.

Serves 4
450g/1lb red plums
300ml/½ pint/1¼ cups apple
  juice
2 egg whites
30ml/2 tbsp concentrated apple
  juice syrup
freshly grated nutmeg, to serve

1 Halve the plums and remove the stones (pits). Place them in a wide pan, with the apple juice.

2 Bring to the boil, then cover with a lid and leave to simmer gently for 20–30 minutes or until the plums are tender.

3 Place the egg whites in a grease-free, dry bowl and whisk until they form soft peaks.

4 Gradually whisk in the apple juice syrup, whisking until the meringue holds fairly firm peaks.

5 Using a tablespoon, scoop the meringue mixture into the gently simmering plum sauce. You may need to cook the "islands" in two batches.

6 Cover and allow to simmer gently for 2–3 minutes, until the meringues are just set. Serve immediately, sprinkled with a little freshly grated nutmeg.

Cook's Tips
• To make a neatly shaped "island", scoop up a round of beaten egg white and lightly mould into an oval shape using two spoons before placing in the simmering sauce.
• A bottle of concentrated apple juice is a useful store-cupboard (pantry) sweetener, but if you don't have any, use a little honey instead.

Caribbean Bananas Energy 310Kcal/1311kJ; Protein 2.9g; Carbohydrate 66g, of which sugars 61.4g; Fat 3.7g, of which saturates 1.1g; Cholesterol 0mg; Calcium 25mg; Fibre 2.2g; Sodium 52mg.
Mulled Pears Energy 233Kcal/982kJ; Protein 1.3g; Carbohydrate 41.5g, of which sugars 41.4g; Fat 1.9g, of which saturates 0.1g; Cholesterol 0mg; Calcium 43mg; Fibre 3.5g; Sodium 12mg.
Floating Islands Energy 97Kcal/417kJ; Protein 2.2g; Carbohydrate 23.3g, of which sugars 23.3g; Fat 0.2g, of which saturates 0g; Cholesterol 0mg; Calcium 22mg; Fibre 1.8g; Sodium 55mg.

Grilled Nectarines with Ricotta & Spice

An irresistibly delicious combination of fresh nectarines and smooth ricotta cheese flavoured with star anise, this fresh fruit dessert can be put together in minutes. Canned peach halves can be used if fresh ones are not available.

Serves 4

4 ripe nectarines or peaches
15ml/1 tbsp light muscovado (brown) sugar
115g/4oz/½ cup ricotta cheese or fromage frais
2.5ml/½ tsp ground star anise

1 Cut the nectarines in half and remove the stones (pits).

2 Arrange the nectarines, cut side upwards, in a wide flameproof dish or on a baking sheet.

3 Stir the sugar into the ricotta or fromage frais. Using a teaspoon, carefully spoon the mixture into the hollow of each nectarine half.

4 Sprinkle with the star anise. Place under a moderately hot grill (broiler) for 6–8 minutes, or until the nectarines are hot and bubbling. Serve warm.

Cook's Tips
• Star anise has a warm, rich flavour that instantly imparts a distinctive Oriental touch to all kinds of dessert dishes. Try making a fruit and star anise jam to make a tasty topping for grilled (broiled) fruit and pancakes or muffins. Simply simmer some fruits of your choice with sugar, fruit juices, a little fruit rind, spices to taste and a couple of star anise. Melon works particularly well with star anise. Store the jam cold in sterilized jars, or serve up immediately.
• If you can't obtain star anise, try ground cloves or mixed (apple pie) spice instead.

Cherry Pancakes

These pancakes are virtually fat free, and lower in calories and higher in fibre than traditional ones. They also freeze well, which is handy – layer the pancakes, separated by waxed paper, before freezing.

Serves 4

50g/2oz/½ cup plain (all-purpose) flour
50g/2oz/½ cup plain wholemeal (all-purpose whole-wheat) flour
pinch of salt
1 egg white
150ml/¼ pint/⅔ cup skimmed milk
150ml/¼ pint/⅔ cup water
a little oil, for frying

For the filling
425g/15oz can black cherries in juice
7.5ml/1½ tsp arrowroot

1 Sift the flours and salt into a bowl, adding any bran left in the sieve (strainer) to the bowl at the end.

2 Make a well in the centre of the flour and add the egg white. Gradually beat in the milk and the water, whisking hard until all the liquid is incorporated and the batter is smooth and bubbly.

3 Heat a non-stick pan with a small amount of oil until the pan is very hot. Pour in just enough batter to cover the base of the pan, swirling the pan to cover the base evenly.

4 Cook until the pancake is set and golden, and then turn to cook the other side. Remove to a sheet of kitchen paper and then cook the remaining batter to make about eight pancakes.

5 Drain the cherries, reserving the juice. Blend about 30ml/ 2 tbsp of the juice from the can of cherries with the arrowroot in a pan. Stir in the rest of the juice. Heat gently, stirring, until boiling. Stir over a moderate heat for about 2 minutes, until thickened and clear.

6 Add the cherries and stir until thoroughly heated. Spoon the cherries into the pancakes and fold them into quarters.

Grilled Nectarines Energy 118Kcal/499kJ; Protein 4.5g; Carbohydrate 16.5g, of which sugars 16.5g; Fat 4.3g, of which saturates 2.6g; Cholesterol 12mg; Calcium 11mg; Fibre 1.6g; Sodium 2mg.
Cherry Pancakes Energy 200Kcal/852kJ; Protein 4.9g; Carbohydrate 40.7g, of which sugars 21.7g; Fat 3.2g, of which saturates 0.4g; Cholesterol 1mg; Calcium 97mg; Fibre 1.4g; Sodium 41mg.

Crunchy Gooseberry Crumble

Combining gooseberries with an oat and nut crumble topping gives this popular family pudding a high-fibre slant. The result is a dessert that will both satisfy and delight everyone.

Serves 4

500g/1¼lb/5 cups gooseberries
50g/2oz/4 tbsp caster
(superfine) sugar

75g/3oz/scant 1 cup rolled oats
75g/3oz/⅔ cup wholemeal
(whole-wheat) flour
60ml/4 tbsp sunflower oil
50g/2oz/4 tbsp demerara
(raw) sugar
30ml/2 tbsp chopped walnuts
low-fat natural (plain) yogurt or
custard, to serve

1 Preheat the oven to 200°C/400°F/Gas 6. Place the gooseberries in a pan with the caster sugar. Cover the pan and cook over a low heat for 10 minutes, until the gooseberries are just tender. Transfer to an ovenproof dish.

2 Make the crumble. Place the oats, flour and oil in a bowl and stir with a fork until evenly mixed.

3 Stir in the demerara sugar and walnuts, then spread evenly over the gooseberries. Bake for 25–30 minutes, or until golden and bubbling. Serve hot with yogurt, or custard made with skimmed milk.

> **Cook's Tip**
> *The best gooseberries to use are the early cooking varieties, which are firm and green with a sour taste. The eating gooseberries vary more in colour and usually have softer flesh.*

> **Variation**
> *When gooseberries are out of season, try making this crumble with other fruits such as apples, plums or rhubarb.*

Tofu Berry "Cheesecake"

This summery "cheesecake" is a light and refreshing finish to any meal. Strictly speaking, it is not really a cheesecake at all, as it is based on tofu – but who would guess?

Serves 6

50g/2oz/4 tbsp low-fat spread
30ml/2 tbsp apple juice
115g/4oz/6 cups bran flakes or
other high-fibre cereal

For the filling
275g/10oz/1¼ cups tofu or
skimmed-milk soft cheese

200g/7oz/scant 1 cup low-fat
natural (plain) yogurt
15ml/1 tbsp/1 sachet powdered
gelatine
60ml/4 tbsp apple juice

For the topping
175g/6oz/1¾ cups mixed
summer soft fruit, such as
strawberries, raspberries,
redcurrants, blackberries, etc.
(or frozen "fruits of the forest")
30ml/2 tbsp redcurrant jelly
30ml/2 tbsp hot water

1 For the base, place the low-fat spread and apple juice in a pan and heat them gently until the spread has melted. Crush the cereal and stir it into the pan.

2 Turn into a 23cm/9in round flan tin (tart pan) and press down firmly. Leave to set.

3 Make the filling. Place the tofu or cheese and yogurt in a blender or food processor and process until smooth. Dissolve the gelatine in the apple juice and stir the juice immediately into the tofu mixture.

4 Spread the tofu mixture over the chilled cereal base, smoothing it evenly. Place in the refrigerator until the filling is firm and set.

5 Remove the flan tin and transfer the cheesecake to a serving plate. Arrange the mixed summer fruits over the top. Melt the redcurrant jelly with the hot water to make a glaze, allow it cool, then spoon over the fruit and serve.

Gooseberry Crumble Energy 406Kcal/1706kJ; Protein 7.3g; Carbohydrate 55.8g, of which sugars 30.5g; Fat 18.7g, of which saturates 1.8g; Cholesterol 0mg; Calcium 73mg; Fibre 6.2g; Sodium 11mg.
Tofu "Cheesecake" Energy 175Kcal/735kJ; Protein 8.1g; Carbohydrate 23.2g, of which sugars 13.7g; Fat 6.1g, of which saturates 1.4g; Cholesterol 1mg; Calcium 314mg; Fibre 2.8g; Sodium 241mg.

Three-Fruit Compote

A combination of dried and fresh fruit, flavoured with fragrant orange flower water, makes a super-fast, refreshing dessert. Using a melon-baller gives the compote a classy touch, but you could always cut the melon into cubes if you find it quicker.

Serves 6
175g/6oz/³⁄₄ cup ready-to-eat, dried apricots
300ml/¹⁄₂ pint/1¹⁄₄ cups water
1 small ripe pineapple
1 small ripe melon
15ml/1 tbsp orange flower water
fresh sprig of mint, to decorate

1 Put the apricots in a medium pan with the water. Bring to the boil, then simmer for 5 minutes. Transfer to a serving bowl and set aside to cool.

2 Peel and quarter the pineapple, then cut the core from each quarter and discard. Cut the flesh into chunks. Reserve any juices that collect.

3 Seed the melon and scoop balls from the flesh, again saving any juices that collect. Pour all the reserved fruit juices into the bowl of apricots with the orange flower water.

4 Add the pineapple and melon pieces to the bowl and mix well together. Chill the fruit salad lightly and decorate with mint just before serving.

> **Variation**
> *A good fruit salad needn't be a boring mixture of multi-coloured fruits swimming in sweet syrup. Instead of the usual apple, orange and grape type of salad, give it a theme, such as red berry fruits or a variety of sliced green fruits – even a dish of just one fruit nicely prepared and sprinkled lightly with some sugar and fresh lemon juice can look beautiful and tastes delicious. Do not use more than three fruits in a salad, so that the flavours remain distinct.*

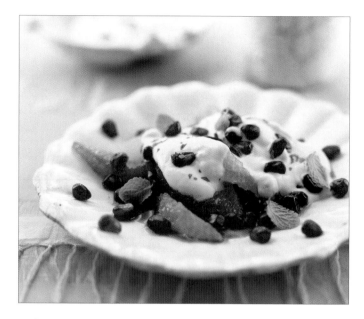

Minted Pomegranate Yogurt

In this simple Moroccan recipe, the juicy, ruby seeds of pomegranates and tangy mint are added to plain yogurt to make a flavourful light dessert. The dish is fabulous served with a citrus fruit salad (as shown in the picture).

Serves 3–4
300ml/¹⁄₂ pint/1¹⁄₄ cups Greek (US strained plain) yogurt
2 or 3 ripe pomegranates
small bunch of fresh mint, finely chopped
honey or sugar, to taste (optional)
handful of pomegranate seeds and mint leaves, to decorate

1 Put the yogurt in a bowl and beat well. Cut open the pomegranates and scoop out the seeds, removing all the bitter pith. Fold the pomegranate seeds and chopped mint into the yogurt. Sweeten with a little honey or sugar, if using, then chill.

2 To serve, decorate the chilled yogurt with a sprinkling of pomegranate seeds and mint leaves.

Blackberries in Port

Pour this rich fruit compote over ice cream or serve it with a spoonful of clotted cream to create an attractive, rich dessert. Taking only minutes to make, it provides the perfect end to a dinner party.

Serves 4
300ml/¹⁄₂ pint/1¹⁄₄ cups ruby port
75g/3oz/6 tbsp caster (superfine) sugar
150ml/¹⁄₄ pint/²⁄₃ cup water
450g/1lb/4 cups fresh blackberries

1 Pour the port into a pan, then add the sugar and water. Stir over a gentle heat with a wooden spoon until the sugar has completely dissolved.

2 Remove the pan from the heat and stir in the blackberries. Set aside to cool, then pour into a bowl and cover with clear film (plastic wrap). Chill until ready to serve.

Three-Fruit Compote Energy 94Kcal/399kJ; Protein 1.9g; Carbohydrate 22.1g, of which sugars 22.1g; Fat 0.4g, of which saturates 0g; Cholesterol 0mg; Calcium 44mg; Fibre 3g; Sodium 31mg.
Pomegranate Yogurt Energy 103Kcal/430kJ; Protein 5.4g; Carbohydrate 5.1g, of which sugars 4.4g; Fat 7.8g, of which saturates 3.9g; Cholesterol 0mg; Calcium 140mg; Fibre 0.5g; Sodium 56mg.
Blackberries in Port Energy 220Kcal/924kJ; Protein 1.2g; Carbohydrate 34.3g, of which sugars 34.3g; Fat 0.2g, of which saturates 0g; Cholesterol 0mg; Calcium 59mg; Fibre 3.5g; Sodium 7mg.

Peach, Blackberry & Ice Cream Gratin

A wonderfully easy dessert in which the flavours of the peaches, blackberries, ice cream and brown sugar mingle together as they cook. Use large, ripe peaches to allow enough space for the filling.

Serves 4

4 large peaches
15ml/1 tbsp lemon juice
120ml/4fl oz/½ cup vanilla
   ice cream
115g/4oz/1 cup small
   blackberries
40g/1½oz/3 tbsp light
   muscovado (brown)
   sugar

1 Preheat the grill (broiler). Cut the peaches in half and remove the stones (pits). Cut a thin slice off the rounded side of each peach so that they sit flat on the surface.

2 Brush the cut surfaces with lemon juice and transfer to a shallow flameproof dish. Grill (broil) for 2 minutes. Remove from the heat; leave the grill on to maintain the temperature.

3 Using a small teaspoon, take small scoops of the ice cream and pack them into the peach halves, piling up in the centre. Add the blackberries, pushing them gently into the ice cream.

4 Sprinkle the filled peaches with the muscovado sugar and grill for a further 1–2 minutes until the sugar has dissolved and the ice cream is beginning to melt. Serve immediately.

Cook's Tips
• *Don't take the ice cream out of the freezer until just before you are ready to fill the peaches, and then work quickly. The ice cream must still be solid or it will melt too quickly when the dessert is under the hot grill (broiler).*
• *Other berries, such as fresh blueberries, can be used instead of blackberries, if you prefer.*

Pineapple Crush Ice Cream

Look out for pineapples that are labelled "extra sweet". This type has bright yellow flesh that is naturally sweet and juicy, and is ideal for this easy-to-make ice cream.

Serves 4–6

2 extra-sweet pineapples
50g/2oz/¼ cup caster
   (superfine) sugar
300ml/½ pint/1¼ cups
   whipping cream

1 Slice one pineapple in half lengthways through the leafy top, then scoop out the flesh from both halves, keeping the shells intact. Reserve the flesh. Stand the shells upside down to drain, wrap in clear film (plastic wrap) and chill until needed.

2 Trim the top off the remaining pineapple, cut the flesh into slices, then cut away the skin and any eyes. Remove the core from each slice, then finely chop the flesh from both pineapples. Purée 300g/11oz of the pineapple in a food processor or blender, reserving the remaining pineapple.

3 Using an ice-cream maker, churn the pineapple purée with the sugar for 15–20 minutes. Mix in the cream and churn until thick but too soft to scoop.

4 Add 175g/6oz/1½ cups of the chopped pineapple and continue to churn the ice cream until it is stiff enough to serve in scoops. Serve, offering any remaining pineapple separately.

Cook's Tip
To make the ice cream by hand, whip the cream until it is just thick. Fold in the purée and sugar, then freeze for 6 hours, beating twice. Fold in the pineapple and freeze for 2–3 hours.

Variation
This is also delicious mixed with meringues: crumble four meringue nests into the mixture when adding the pineapple.

Ice Cream Gratin Energy 138Kcal/583kJ; Protein 2.4g; Carbohydrate 26.8g, of which sugars 26.4g; Fat 2.8g, of which saturates 1.8g; Cholesterol 7mg; Calcium 55mg; Fibre 2.4g; Sodium 20mg.
Pineapple Ice Cream Energy 278Kcal/1159kJ; Protein 1.6g; Carbohydrate 23.5g, of which sugars 23.5g; Fat 20.4g, of which saturates 12.6g; Cholesterol 53mg; Calcium 58mg; Fibre 1.6g; Sodium 16mg.

Yogurt with Apricots & Pistachios

Add subtly honeyed apricots and chopped pistachio nuts to creamy yogurt and you have a dessert with a really distinctive and exotic flavour. This truly is an instant dish that can be whipped up in next to no time, and you can easily vary it, to taste, with whatever ingredients you happen to have to hand.

Serves 4
450g/1lb/2 cups Greek (US strained plain) yogurt
175g/6oz/³⁄₄ cup ready-to-eat dried apricots, chopped
15ml/1 tbsp clear honey
grated rind of ¹⁄₂ orange
30ml/2 tbsp unsalted pistachios, roughly chopped
ground cinnamon

1 Place the dried apricots in a pan, barely cover with water and simmer for just 3 minutes, to soften.

2 Drain the apricots and transfer to a bowl. Allow to cool, then mix with the honey.

3 Mix the yogurt with the apricots, orange rind and nuts.

4 Spoon into sundae dishes, sprinkle over a little cinnamon and chill until ready to serve.

Cook's Tip
Straining the yogurt overnight will make the dessert thicker, if you prefer that consistency, although this obviously requires advance planning and so means that the dish is no longer a really quick, last-minute option. To strain the yogurt, simply leave it in a sieve (strainer) over a bowl in the refrigerator overnight. The next day, discard the liquid whey collected from the yogurt.

Variation
Sprinkle over a little demerara (raw) sugar or grated chocolate with the ground cinnamon for added flavour.

Raspberry Yogurt Layer

If you are looking for a really speedy and healthy dessert, then this is the one for you. Low in fat and high in fibre, it is packed with goodness. Try it for your breakfast, too.

Serves 4
225g/8oz/1¹⁄₃ cups fresh or frozen and thawed raspberries
225g/8oz/1 cup low-fat natural (plain) yogurt
75g/3oz/³⁄₄ cup Swiss-style muesli (granola)

1 Reserve four raspberries for decoration, and then spoon a few raspberries into four stemmed glasses or glass dishes.

2 Top the raspberries with a spoonful of yogurt in each glass.

3 Sprinkle a generous layer of muesli over the yogurt. Now repeat with the raspberries and other ingredients. Top each with a whole raspberry.

Cook's Tips
• This recipe can be made in advance and stored in the refrigerator for several hours without spoiling.
• Muesli is made up of a mix of cereal, dried fruit and nuts and is therefore high in fibre. When buying muesli from the wide range available in stores, choose a type that is low in sugar to keep in tune with the healthy feel of the dish.

Variations
• This recipe can be made with whatever fruit is in season. Fresh strawberries, redcurrants or peaches would all taste delicious as would tropical fruit such as mango and banana. Layers of cooked, puréed apple or lightly poached plums also make a tasty substitute for the raspberries. For a last-minute dessert, canned fruit would be perfectly acceptable.
• Instead of layers of muesli, try crushed digestive biscuits (graham crackers) or ginger nut biscuits (gingersnaps).

Yogurt with Apricots Energy 255Kcal/1064kJ; Protein 10.3g; Carbohydrate 21.7g, of which sugars 21.5g; Fat 15.9g, of which saturates 6.4g; Cholesterol 0mg; Calcium 209mg; Fibre 3.2g; Sodium 126mg.
Raspberry Muesli Energy 114Kcal/483kJ; Protein 5.5g; Carbohydrate 20.4g, of which sugars 11.7g; Fat 2g, of which saturates 0.5g; Cholesterol 1mg; Calcium 142mg; Fibre 2.6g; Sodium 120mg.

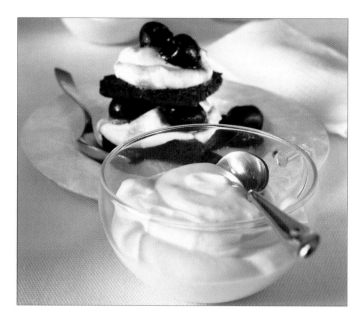

Coffee Mascarpone Creams

For the best results, use good quality coffee beans and make the coffee as strong as possible. These little desserts are very rich so you need a really robust shot of coffee to give the desired result. They are particularly good served with a glass of liqueur or a cup of espresso.

Serves 4
115g/4oz/½ cup mascarpone
45ml/3 tbsp strong espresso
  coffee
45g/1¾oz/3 tbsp icing
  (confectioners') sugar
500g/1¼lb/5 cups cherries

1 Put the mascarpone in a bowl and add the coffee. Mix well until smooth and creamy. Sift in the icing sugar and stir until thoroughly combined.

2 Spoon the mixture into little china pots or ramekin dishes and top with the cherries. Chill for 30 minutes before serving.

Cook's Tip
Chocolate-dipped strawberries make a lovely accompaniment to these desserts. Melt some broken-up chocolate in a small deep heatproof bowl set over a pan of barely simmering water. While the chocolate is melting, line a baking sheet with baking parchment. Stir the melted chocolate until it is completely smooth. Holding a strawberry by its stalk, dip it partially or fully into the melted chocolate, allowing any excess chocolate to drip off, then place the fruit on the baking sheet. Repeat with the rest of the fruit. Leave to set and use on the same day.

Variation
You can flavour mascarpone with almost anything you like to make a quick but elegant dessert. Try replacing the coffee with the same quantity of orange juice, Marsala or honey.

Chocolate Banana Fools

This de luxe version of banana custard looks great served in glasses. Quick to put together, it can be made a few hours in advance and chilled until ready to serve.

Serves 4
115g/4oz plain (semisweet)
  chocolate, chopped
300ml/½ pint/1¼ cups
  fresh custard
2 bananas

1 Put the chocolate in a heatproof bowl and melt in the microwave on High for 1–2 minutes. Stir, then set aside to cool. Alternatively, put the chocolate in a heatproof bowl, set it over a pan of simmering water and leave until melted, stirring frequently.

2 Pour the custard into a bowl and gently fold in the melted chocolate to make a rippled effect.

3 Peel and slice the bananas and stir these into the chocolate and custard mixture. Spoon into four glasses and chill for 30 minutes–1 hour before serving.

Lemon Posset

This creamy dessert dates back to the Middle Ages.

Serves 4
600ml/1 pint/2½ cups double
  (heavy) cream

175g/6oz/¾ cup caster (superfine)
  sugar
grated rind and juice of
  2 unwaxed lemons

1 Gently heat the cream and sugar together in a pan until the sugar has dissolved, then bring to the boil, stirring constantly.

2 Add the lemon juice and rind to the cream mixture and stir until it thickens.

3 Pour the posset into four heatproof serving glasses and chill until just set, then serve.

Coffee Creams Energy 96Kcal/403kJ; Protein 2.7g; Carbohydrate 12.7g, of which sugars 12.7g; Fat 4.2g, of which saturates 2.6g; Cholesterol 12mg; Calcium 6mg; Fibre 0g; Sodium 1mg.
Banana Fools Energy 263Kcal/1106kJ; Protein 4g; Carbohydrate 40.9g, of which sugars 37g; Fat 9.5g, of which saturates 4.9g; Cholesterol 3mg; Calcium 81mg; Fibre 1.3g; Sodium 33mg.
Lemon Posset Energy 917Kcal/3797kJ; Protein 2.6g; Carbohydrate 48.3g, of which sugars 48.3g; Fat 80.6g, of which saturates 50.1g; Cholesterol 206mg; Calcium 97mg; Fibre 0g; Sodium 36mg.

Banana & Passion Fruit Whip

This very easy and quickly prepared dessert has a delicious tropical flavour. Serve with dainty, crisp biscuits (cookies) for a lovely contrast to the creamy texture.

Serves 4

2 ripe bananas
2 passion fruit
115g/4oz/½ cup fromage frais or mascarpone
150ml/¼ pint/⅔ cup double (heavy) cream
10ml/2 tsp clear honey

1 Peel the bananas, then mash them with a fork in a bowl to a smooth purée.

2 Halve the passion fruit and scoop out the pulp. Mix with the bananas and fromage frais. Whip the cream with the honey until it forms soft peaks.

3 Carefully fold the cream and honey mixture into the fruit mixture. Spoon into four glass dishes and serve immediately.

Frudités with Honey Dip

A colourful and tasty variation on the popular savoury crudités, this dessert is great fun for impromptu entertaining.

Serves 4

225g/8oz/1 cup Greek (US strained plain) yogurt
45ml/3 tbsp clear honey
selection of fresh fruit for dipping such as apples, pears, tangerines, grapes, figs, cherries, strawberries and kiwi fruit

1 Place the yogurt in a dish, beat until smooth, then partially stir in the honey, leaving a slight marbled effect.

2 Cut the various fruits into wedges or bite-size pieces or leave whole. Arrange the fruits on a platter with the bowl of dip in the centre. Serve chilled.

Quick Apricot Blender Whip

One of the speediest desserts you could make – as well as being one of the prettiest. Perfect for mid-week meals when you have run out of time.

Serves 4

400g/14oz can apricot halves in juice
15ml/1 tbsp Grand Marnier or brandy
175g/6oz/¾ cup Greek (US strained plain) yogurt
30ml/2 tbsp flaked (sliced) almonds

1 Drain the juice from the apricots and place the fruit and liqueur in a blender or food processor. Process the apricots to a smooth purée.

2 Spoon the fruit purée and yogurt in alternate spoonfuls into four tall glasses or glass dishes, swirling them together slightly to give a marbled effect.

3 Lightly toast the almonds in a dry, non-stick frying pan or under the grill (broiler) until they are golden. Allow them to cool slightly, then sprinkle them over the top of the desserts.

Cook's Tips
• Why not make quick petit four biscuits (cookies) to serve with this fruit whip? Roll out a carton of chocolate chip cookie dough on a floured surface to 1cm/½in thick. Using a small pastry (cookie) cutter, stamp out as many rounds as possible and transfer to a lightly greased baking sheet. Bake according to the packet instructions and leave to cool. Meanwhile, melt some plain (semisweet) chocolate in a bowl set over a pan of simmering water, then allow to cool. Use the chocolate to sandwich together the biscuits in pairs, then serve. These are delicious with any creamy dessert.
• For an even lighter dessert, use low-fat yogurt instead of Greek (US strained plain) yogurt, and replace the liqueur with a little fruit juice from the can of apricots.

Fruit Whip Energy 262Kcal/1086kJ; Protein 2.5g; Carbohydrate 15.4g, of which sugars 14.3g; Fat 21.6g, of which saturates 13.4g; Cholesterol 56mg; Calcium 41mg; Fibre 0.7g; Sodium 18mg.
Frudités Energy 141Kcal/595kJ; Protein 4g; Carbohydrate 20.9g, of which sugars 20.9g; Fat 5.9g, of which saturates 2.9g; Cholesterol 0mg; Calcium 90mg; Fibre 2g; Sodium 44mg.
Apricot Whip Energy 168Kcal/701kJ; Protein 4.8g; Carbohydrate 17.5g, of which sugars 17.3g; Fat 8.8g, of which saturates 2.6g; Cholesterol 0mg; Calcium 103mg; Fibre 1.5g; Sodium 42mg.

Brazilian Coffee Bananas

Rich and sinful-looking, this tasty dessert takes only about two minutes to make – just the job for a busy modern lifestyle.

Serves 4

4 small ripe bananas
15ml/1 tbsp instant coffee
   granules or powder
15ml/1 tbsp hot water
25g/1oz/2 tbsp dark muscovado
   (molasses) sugar
250g/9oz/1⅛ cups Greek (US
   strained plain) yogurt
15ml/1 tbsp toasted flaked
   (sliced) almonds

1 Peel and slice one banana and roughly mash the remaining three with a fork.

2 Dissolve the coffee in the hot water, then stir into the mashed bananas.

3 Spoon a little of the mashed banana mixture into four individual dishes and sprinkle with sugar. Top with a spoonful of yogurt, then repeat until all the ingredients are used up.

4 Swirl the last layer of yogurt for a marbled effect. Finish with a few banana slices and flaked almonds. Serve immediately – if possible, serve within about an hour of making.

> **Cook's Tip**
> *Sprinkle the sliced banana, for the topping, with freshly squeezed lemon juice to prevent it from turning brown.*

> **Variations**
> *For a special occasion, add a dash of dark rum or brandy to the bananas for extra richness. Chocolate teams up with coffee and banana very well, so for a luxurious touch, drizzle some melted chocolate over the sliced banana and nut topping.*

Figs with Ricotta Cream

Fresh, ripe figs are full of natural sweetness, and need little adornment. This simple recipe really makes the most of their beautiful, intense flavour.

Serves 4

4 ripe, fresh figs
115g/4oz/¼ cup ricotta or
   cottage cheese
45ml/3 tbsp crème fraîche
15ml/1 tbsp clear honey
2.5ml/½ tsp vanilla extract
freshly grated nutmeg, to decorate

1 Trim the stalks from the figs. Make four cuts through each fig from the stalk-end, cutting almost right through but leaving them intact at the base. Place on serving plates and open them out.

2 Mix together the ricotta or cottage cheese, crème fraîche, honey and vanilla.

3 Spoon a little ricotta cream on to each plate and sprinkle with grated nutmeg to serve.

Red Fruit Coulis with Meringue

A heavenly, vibrant sauce teamed with crisp meringue.

Serves 6

225g/8oz/2 cups redcurrants,
   removed from stalks
450g/1lb/2⅔ cups raspberries
50g/2oz/½ cup icing
   (confectioners') sugar
15ml/1 tbsp cornflour (cornstarch)
juice of 1 orange
6 ready-made meringues
double (heavy) cream, to serve

1 Place the fruit in a food processor or blender with the sugar and purée. Press through a fine sieve (strainer).

2 Blend the cornflour with the orange juice, then stir into the fruit purée. Transfer to a pan, simmer for 1–2 minutes, stirring, until smooth and thick. Cool, then spoon some coulis on to individual plates, swirl in a little cream and top with a meringue.

Coffee Bananas Energy 210Kcal/882kJ; Protein 5.9g; Carbohydrate 30.2g, of which sugars 28.1g; Fat 8.7g, of which saturates 3.5g; Cholesterol 0mg; Calcium 112mg; Fibre 1.3g; Sodium 46mg.
Figs with Ricotta Cream Energy 128Kcal/536kJ; Protein 4.6g; Carbohydrate 14.6g, of which sugars 14.6g; Fat 6g, of which saturates 3.7g; Cholesterol 17mg; Calcium 93mg; Fibre 1.5g; Sodium 102mg.
Red Fruit Coulis Energy 138Kcal/589kJ; Protein 2.4g; Carbohydrate 33.7g, of which sugars 31.4g; Fat 0.3g, of which saturates 0.1g; Cholesterol 0mg; Calcium 49mg; Fibre 3.2g; Sodium 25mg.

Prune & Orange Pots

A handy storecupboard dessert, made in minutes. It can be served straight away, but for the best effect, chill for about half an hour before serving.

Serves 4
225g/8oz/1 cup ready-to-eat dried prunes
150ml/¼ pint/⅔ cup orange juice
225g/8oz/1 cup low-fat natural (plain) yogurt
shredded, pared orange rind, to decorate

1 Remove the pits from the prunes and roughly chop the flesh. Put the prunes in a pan with the orange juice.

2 Bring the juice to the boil, stirring. Reduce the heat, cover and leave to simmer for 5 minutes, until the prunes are tender and the liquid is reduced by half.

3 Remove from the heat, allow to cool slightly and then beat well with a wooden spoon, until the fruit breaks down to a rough purée.

4 Transfer the mixture to a bowl. Stir in the yogurt, swirling the yogurt and fruit purée together lightly, to give an attractive marbled effect.

5 Spoon the mixture into stemmed glasses or individual dishes, smoothing the tops.

6 Top each dish with a few shreds of orange rind, to decorate. Chill before serving.

Variations
This dessert can also be made with other ready-to-eat dried fruit, such as apricots or peaches. For a special occasion, add a dash of brandy or Cointreau with the yogurt. Sprinkle the top of each serving with toasted flaked (sliced) almonds or crumbled amaretti to give added texture to the dessert.

Fresh Pineapple Salad

A fragrant and fresh-tasting fruit salad, this dessert can be prepared very quickly, ahead of time. Orange flower water gives the salad its special quality – it is available from Middle Eastern food stores or good delicatessens.

Serves 4
1 small ripe pineapple
icing (confectioners') sugar, to taste
15ml/1 tbsp orange flower water, or more to taste
115g/4oz/generous ½ cup fresh dates, stoned (pitted) and quartered
225g/8oz/2 cups fresh strawberries, sliced
few fresh mint sprigs, to decorate

1 Peel the pineapple and, using the tip of a vegetable peeler, remove as many brown "eyes" as possible.

2 Cut the peeled pineapple into quarters, lengthways, remove the core, then slice.

3 Arrange the pineapple slices in a shallow glass bowl that is large enough to accommodate the dates and strawberries added in the next step. Sprinkle with the icing sugar and the orange flower water.

4 Add the dates and strawberries to the pineapple, cover and chill for at least 2 hours, stirring once or twice.

5 Serve the fruit salad slightly chilled, decorated with a few mint sprigs.

Cook's Tip
Make sure that the dates you use are of a good enough quality or they could spoil the dish. Fresh dates should be plump with smooth, shiny brown skins. The flesh ought to have a rich, honey-like flavour and dense texture.

Prune & Orange Pots Energy 124Kcal/528kJ; Protein 4.5g; Carbohydrate 26.7g, of which sugars 26.7g; Fat 0.8g, of which saturates 0.3g; Cholesterol 1mg; Calcium 130mg; Fibre 3.3g; Sodium 57mg.
Pineapple Salad Energy 92Kcal/391kJ; Protein 1.3g; Carbohydrate 22.4g, of which sugars 22.4g; Fat 0.3g, of which saturates 0g; Cholesterol 0mg; Calcium 34mg; Fibre 2.3g; Sodium 7mg.

Grapefruit in Honey & Whisky

Create a simple yet elegant dessert by arranging a colourful fan of pink, red and white grapefruit segments in a sweet whisky sauce. This dessert is perfect after a rich meal.

Serves 4

1 pink grapefruit
1 red grapefruit
1 white grapefruit
50g/2oz/^{1}/4 cup sugar
150ml/^{1}/4 pint/^{2}/3 cup water
60ml/4 tbsp clear honey
45ml/3 tbsp whisky
fresh mint sprigs, to decorate

1 Cut a thin slice from each end of the grapefruits. Place cut side down on a plate and cut off the peel and pith in strips. Remove any remaining pith.

2 Cut out each segment, leaving the membrane behind. Put the segments into a shallow bowl.

3 Put the sugar and water into a heavy pan, bring to the boil, stirring constantly, until the sugar has dissolved, then simmer, without stirring, for 10 minutes, until thickened and syrupy.

4 Heat the honey in a pan and boil until it becomes a slightly deeper colour or begins to caramelize.

5 Remove the pan from the heat, add the whisky and, using a match or taper, carefully ignite, if you like, then pour the mixture into the sugar syrup.

6 Bring to the boil, and pour over the fruit. Cover and leave until cold. To serve, arrange the grapefruit segments on individual plates, alternating the colours, and pour over the syrup. Add the mint.

> **Variation**
> The whisky can be replaced with brandy, Cointreau or Grand Marnier, any of which will work just as well.

Watermelon, Ginger & Grapefruit Salad

This pretty pink salad ably proves that a dish doesn't need to be complicated to taste great. Here, sweet stem ginger brilliantly ties together the freshness of the watermelon and the tang of the grapefruit.

Serves 4

500g/1^1/4lb/2 cups diced watermelon flesh
2 red or pink grapefruit
2 pieces preserved stem ginger, plus 30ml/2 tbsp of the preserved stem ginger syrup
whipped cream, to serve

1 Remove any seeds from the watermelon with a knife and cut into bitesize chunks. Place in a serving bowl.

2 Cut a thin slice from each end of the grapefruit. Place cut side down on a plate and, using a sharp knife, cut off the peel and pith in strips. Remove any remaining pith. Cut out each segment, leaving the membrane behind; catch any juice in a bowl as you work.

3 Add the grapefruit segments and collected juice to the bowl of watermelon. Finely chop the stem ginger and add to the fruits in the bowl.

4 Spoon over the ginger syrup and toss the fruits lightly in the syrup to mix evenly. Chill before serving with a bowl of whipped cream.

> **Cook's Tip**
> Toss the fruits gently, otherwise the grapefruit segments will break up and the appearance of the dish will be spoiled.

> **Variation**
> Use blood oranges instead of the grapefruit and add orange rind shreds with the ginger.

Rhubarb & Ginger Trifles

Choose a good-quality jar of rhubarb compote for this speedy recipe; try to find one with large, chunky pieces of fruit.

Serves 4
12 ginger nut biscuits
   (gingersnaps)
50ml/2fl oz/¼ cup rhubarb
   compote
450ml/¾ pint/scant 2 cups extra
   thick double (heavy) cream

1 Put the ginger biscuits in a plastic bag and seal. Press the biscuits with a rolling pin until roughly crushed.

2 Set aside 30ml/2 tbsp of the crushed biscuits and divide the rest among four glasses.

3 Spoon the rhubarb compote on top of the crushed biscuits, then top with the cream. Place in the refrigerator and chill for about 30 minutes.

4 Sprinkle the reserved crushed biscuits over the trifles and serve immediately.

Scented Red & Orange Fruit Salad

A lovely salad, bursting with colour and exotic tastes.

Serves 4–6
350–400g/12–14oz/3–3½ cups
   strawberries, hulled and halved
3 oranges, peeled and segmented
3 small blood oranges, peeled
   and segmented
1 or 2 passion fruit
120ml/4fl oz/½ cup
   dry white wine
sugar, to taste

1 Put the strawberries and oranges into a serving bowl. Halve the passion fruit and spoon the flesh into the fruit.

2 Pour the wine over the fruit and add sugar to taste. Toss gently, then chill until ready to serve.

Pistachio & Rose Water Oranges

This light and citrusy dessert is perfect to serve after a heavy main course, such as a hearty meat stew or a leg of roast lamb. Combining three favourite Middle Eastern ingredients, the dish is delicately fragrant and refreshing. If pistachio nuts are not available, use hazelnuts instead.

Serves 4
4 large oranges
30ml/2 tbsp rose water
30ml/2 tbsp shelled pistachio
   nuts, roughly chopped

1 Slice the top and bottom off one of the oranges to expose the flesh.

2 Using a small serrated knife, slice down between the pith and the flesh, working round the orange, neatly removing all the peel and pith.

3 Slice the orange horizontally into six rounds, reserving any juice. Repeat with the remaining oranges.

4 Arrange the orange rounds decoratively in a serving dish. Mix the reserved juice with the rose water and drizzle over the oranges.

5 Cover the dish with clear film (plastic wrap) and chill for about 30 minutes. Sprinkle the chopped pistachio nuts over the oranges to serve.

Cook's Tip
Rose-scented sugar is delicious sprinkled over fresh fruit salads. Wash and thoroughly dry a handful of fresh, unsprayed rose petals and place in a sealed container filled with caster (superfine) sugar for 2–3 days. Remove the rose petals, then use the sugar as a delicate flavouring.

Ginger Trifles Energy 695Kcal/2874kJ; Protein 3.6g; Carbohydrate 27.1g, of which sugars 14.1g; Fat 64.3g, of which saturates 39.4g; Cholesterol 154mg; Calcium 98mg; Fibre 0.6g; Sodium 124mg.
Red & Orange Salad Energy 78Kcal/329kJ; Protein 2g; Carbohydrate 14.7g, of which sugars 14.7g; Fat 0.2g, of which saturates 0g; Cholesterol 0mg; Calcium 70mg; Fibre 3g; Sodium 12mg.
Oranges Energy 101Kcal/424kJ; Protein 3g; Carbohydrate 13.4g, of which sugars 13.2g; Fat 4.3g, of which saturates 0.6g; Cholesterol 0mg; Calcium 79mg; Fibre 3g; Sodium 47mg.

Chargrilled Apples on Cinnamon Toasts

This delicious treat provides a truly fabulous finale to any kind of summertime barbecue. However, it can also, just as effectively, be cooked under the grill, which means that you can enjoy it at any time of year.

Serves 4

4 sweet dessert apples
juice of ½ lemon
4 individual English muffins
15ml/1 tbsp low-fat spread, melted
25g/1oz/2 tbsp golden caster (superfine) sugar
5ml/1 tsp ground cinnamon
low-fat Greek (US strained plain) yogurt, to serve (optional)

1 Core all of the dessert apples and then cut them horizontally into three or four thick, equal-sized slices. Sprinkle the slices with the lemon juice.

2 Cut the muffins into halves. Brush sparingly with melted low-fat spread on both sides.

3 Mix together the caster sugar and the ground cinnamon. Preheat the grill (broiler) at this stage if you are not using the barbecue.

4 Place the apple slices and the muffin halves on the hot barbecue – or under the grill – and cook them for about 3–4 minutes, turning once, until they are beginning to turn a golden brown colour.

5 Sprinkle half the cinnamon sugar over the apple slices and muffins and cook for 1 minute more, until they are a rich golden brown.

6 To serve, arrange the apple slices over the toasts and sprinkle them with the remaining cinnamon sugar. Serve hot, with low-fat Greek yogurt, if you like.

Greek Fig & Honey Pudding

This dessert is packed with sunny Greek flavours.

Serves 4

4 fresh or canned figs

2 x 225g/8oz tubs/2 cups Greek (US strained plain) yogurt
60ml/4 tbsp clear honey
30ml/2 tbsp chopped unsalted pistachio nuts

1 Chop the figs and place in the bottom of four stemmed wine glasses or deep, individual dessert bowls.

2 Spoon half a tub (120ml/4fl oz/½ cup) of the thick yogurt on top of the figs in the glasses or bowls. Chill in the refrigerator until ready to serve. Just before serving, drizzle 15ml/1 tbsp of honey over each portion and sprinkle with the pistachio nuts.

Passion Fruit Soufflés

Here, passion fruit adds an exotic twist to a classic.

Serves 4

softened butter, for greasing

200ml/7fl oz/scant 1 cup ready-made fresh custard
3 passion fruit, halved
2 egg whites

1 Preheat the oven to 200°C/400°F/Gas 6. Grease four 200ml/7fl oz/scant 1 cup ramekins or small ovenproof dishes with the butter.

2 Pour the custard into a mixing bowl. Scrape out the seeds and juice from the passion fruit and stir well into the custard.

3 Whisk the egg whites until stiff, and fold a quarter of them into the custard. Carefully fold in the remaining egg whites, then spoon the mixture into the dishes.

4 Place the dishes on a baking sheet and bake in the oven for 8–10 minutes, or until the soufflés are well risen. Serve immediately.

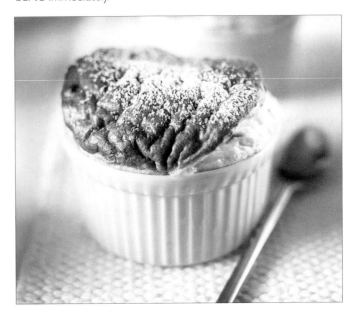

Cinnamon Toasts Energy 218Kcal/926kJ; Protein 5.6g; Carbohydrate 40.9g, of which sugars 17.4g; Fat 4.8g, of which saturates 0.4g; Cholesterol 0mg; Calcium 79mg; Fibre 2.5g; Sodium 92mg.
Greek Fig & Honey Energy 292Kcal/1220kJ; Protein 10.9g; Carbohydrate 25.4g, of which sugars 25.2g; Fat 18.5g, of which saturates 7.7g; Cholesterol 0mg; Calcium 265mg; Fibre 2g; Sodium 152mg.
Fruit Soufflés Energy 59Kcal/249kJ; Protein 3.1g; Carbohydrate 8.8g, of which sugars 7.1g; Fat 1g, of which saturates 0g; Cholesterol 1mg; Calcium 48mg; Fibre 0.4g; Sodium 53mg.

Fruit-Filled Soufflé Omelette

A melt-in-the-mouth dish, this dessert is surprisingly quick to make. The creamy omelette fluffs up in the pan, then is softly folded over to envelop its filling.

Serves 2
75g/3oz/³/4 cup strawberries, hulled
45ml/3 tbsp Kirsch, brandy or Cointreau

3 eggs, separated
25g/1oz/2 tbsp caster (superfine) sugar
45ml/3 tbsp double (heavy) cream, whipped
a few drops of vanilla extract
25g/1oz/2 tbsp butter
icing (confectioners') sugar, sifted

1 Cut the strawberries in half and place in a bowl. Pour over 30ml/2 tbsp of the liqueur and set aside to marinate.

2 Beat the egg yolks and sugar together until pale and fluffy, then fold in the whipped cream and vanilla extract. Whisk the egg whites in a very large, grease-free bowl until stiff, then carefully fold into the yolks.

3 Melt the butter in an omelette pan. When sizzling, pour in the egg mixture and cook until set underneath, shaking occasionally. Spoon on the strawberries and liqueur and, tilting the pan, slide the omelette so that it folds over.

4 Slide the omelette on to a warm plate and spoon over the remaining liqueur. Dredge with icing sugar, cut in half and serve.

Apricot Pancakes

A simple, tasty dessert to keep all the family happy.

Serves 4
115g/4oz/1 cup plain (all-purpose) flour
pinch of salt
1 egg

300ml/½ pint/1¼ cups milk
a little oil, for frying

For the sauce
200g/7oz/scant 1 cup ready-to-eat dried apricots
150ml/¼ pint/⅔ cup apple juice
300ml/½ pint/1¼ cups water

1 Make the sauce. Put the apricots in a pan with the apple juice and water and simmer, covered, for 10 minutes until tender. Cool slightly, then purée in a blender until smooth. Set aside.

2 Sift the flour and salt into a bowl and make a well in the centre. Add the egg and milk and, using a whisk, gradually incorporate the surrounding dry ingredients to form a batter.

3 Heat a lightly oiled, non-stick pan until very hot. Pour in just enough batter to cover the base of the pan, swirling the pan to cover the base evenly. Cook until the pancake is set and golden, and then turn to cook the other side. Keep warm while cooking more pancakes in the same way.

4 Serve the pancakes with the apricot sauce poured over.

Warm Pears in Cider

An easy way of making the most of autumn fruit.

Serves 4
1 lemon
50g/2oz/¼ cup caster (superfine) sugar

a little grated nutmeg
250ml/8fl oz/1 cup sweet (hard) cider
4 firm, ripe pears
freshly made custard, cream or ice cream, to serve

1 Carefully remove the rind from the lemon with a vegetable peeler, leaving any white pith behind.

2 Squeeze the juice from the lemon into a pan large enough to hold the pears. Add the rind, sugar, nutmeg and cider and heat through until the sugar has completely dissolved.

3 Carefully peel the pears, leaving the stalks on if possible, and place in the pan of cider. Poach the pears for 10–15 minutes until almost tender, turning frequently to cook evenly.

4 Transfer the pears to individual serving dishes using a slotted spoon. Simmer the liquid over a high heat until it reduces slightly and becomes syrupy.

5 Pour the warm syrup over the pears, and serve immediately with freshly made custard, cream or ice cream.

Cook's Tip
To get pears of just the right firmness, you may have to buy them slightly under-ripe and then wait a day or more. Soft pears are no good at all for this dish.

Variation
Try using sweet white wine instead of (hard) cider and replace the nutmeg with finely grated orange rind.

Soufflé Omelette Energy 434Kcal/1802kJ; Protein 10.2g; Carbohydrate 18.4g, of which sugars 18.4g; Fat 30.7g, of which saturates 16.4g; Cholesterol 343mg; Calcium 70mg; Fibre 0.4g; Sodium 189mg.
Apricot Pancakes Energy 276Kcal/1168kJ; Protein 7.6g; Carbohydrate 46.1g, of which sugars 24.2g; Fat 8.2g, of which saturates 1.5g; Cholesterol 50mg; Calcium 132mg; Fibre 4.1g; Sodium 42mg.
Pears in Cider Energy 136Kcal/574kJ; Protein 0.5g; Carbohydrate 30.8g, of which sugars 30.8g; Fat 0.2g, of which saturates 0g; Cholesterol 0mg; Calcium 28mg; Fibre 3.3g; Sodium 10mg.

Pineapple Flambé

Flambéing is a quick and tasty way to serve fruit. Setting light to the alcohol gives the dish a delicious, distinctive flavour.

Serves 4
1 large, ripe pineapple
40g/1½oz/3 tbsp unsalted (sweet) butter
40g/1½oz/3 tbsp light soft brown sugar
60ml/4 tbsp fresh orange juice
30ml/2 tbsp brandy or vodka
25g/1oz/4 tbsp slivered (sliced) almonds, toasted
crème fraîche, to serve

1 Slice off the top and base of the pineapple. Then cut down the sides, removing the skin and all the dark "eyes", but leaving the pineapple in a good shape.

2 Cut the pineapple into thin slices and, with an apple corer, remove the hard central core.

3 Heat the butter, sugar and orange juice in a large frying pan until the sugar has dissolved. Add the pineapple slices and cook for about 1–2 minutes, turning once to coat both sides.

4 Add the brandy or vodka and immediately set alight with a long match or taper. Allow the flames to die down and then sprinkle with the toasted almonds. Serve with crème fraîche.

Cook's Tip
If you are serving this dish to children, you can leave out the alcohol – it will taste just as good.

Variation
For speed, use canned pineapple rings in natural juice and replace the orange with the same amount of canned juice.

Grilled Pineapple with Rum Custard

This speedy dessert is perfect for any occasion.

Serves 4
1 ripe pineapple
25g/1oz/2 tbsp butter
fresh strawberries, sliced, to serve
a few pineapple leaves, to decorate

For the sauce
1 egg
2 egg yolks
25g/1oz/2 tbsp caster (superfine) sugar
30ml/2 tbsp dark rum
2.5ml/½ tsp freshly ground black pepper

1 Slice off the top and base of the pineapple. Then cut down the sides, removing the skin and all the dark "eyes", but leaving the pineapple in a good shape.

2 Preheat the grill (broiler) to medium heat. Cut the pineapple into thin slices and, with an apple corer, remove the hard central core. Dot the pineapple slices with butter and grill (broil) for about 5 minutes.

3 Make the sauce. Place all the ingredients in a heatproof bowl. Set over a pan of simmering water and whisk for about 3–4 minutes or until the mixture is foamy and cooked.

4 Scatter the sliced strawberries over the cooked pineapple, decorate with a few pineapple leaves and serve immediately, with the sauce poured over the top of each serving.

Cook's Tips
• The sweetest pineapples are picked and exported when ripe. Contrary to popular belief, pineapples do not ripen well after picking. Choose fruit that smells sweet and yields to firm pressure from your thumbs.
• Freshly ground black pepper may seem an unusual ingredient to team up with pineapple, until you realize that peppercorns are the fruit of a tropical vine. If the idea does not appeal, you can always leave out the pepper – but it's worth a try.

Pineapple Flambé Energy 246Kcal/1032kJ; Protein 2.2g; Carbohydrate 29.9g, of which sugars 29.8g; Fat 12.1g, of which saturates 5.5g; Cholesterol 21mg; Calcium 55mg; Fibre 2.6g; Sodium 67mg.
Grilled Pineapple Energy 203Kcal/853kJ; Protein 3.7g; Carbohydrate 23g, of which sugars 23g; Fat 9.6g, of which saturates 4.4g; Cholesterol 162mg; Calcium 51mg; Fibre 1.8g; Sodium 63mg.

Ginger & Orange Crème Brûlée

With this cheat's version of crème brûlée, the creamy base is set the easy way, without lengthy cooking.

Serves 4–5
2 eggs, plus 2 egg yolks
300ml/½ pint/1¼ cups single (light) cream
25g/1oz/2 tbsp caster (superfine) sugar
5ml/1 tsp powdered gelatine

finely grated rind and juice of ½ orange
1 large piece preserved stem ginger, finely chopped
45–60ml/3–4 tbsp icing (confectioners') or caster (superfine) sugar
orange segments and sprig of mint, to decorate

1 Whisk the eggs and yolks together until pale. Bring the cream and sugar to the boil in a pan, remove from the heat and sprinkle on the gelatine. Stir until the gelatine has dissolved and then pour the cream mixture on to the eggs, whisking constantly.

2 Add the orange rind to the custard, with a little juice to taste, then stir in the chopped ginger.

3 Carefully pour into four or five ramekins or small flameproof dishes and leave in the refrigerator until set.

4 Some time before serving, sprinkle the sugar generously over the top of the custard and put under a very hot grill (broiler). Watch closely for the couple of moments it takes for the tops to caramelize. Allow to cool before serving.

5 Decorate with a few segments of orange and a sprig of mint.

Cook's Tips
• Not many people will guess that this recipe is a cheat – but take care not to over-chill the custard.
• For a milder ginger flavour, just add up to 5ml/1 tsp ground ginger instead of the stem ginger.

Oranges in Hot Coffee Syrup

This easy recipe features an unusual blend of flavours.

Serves 6
6 medium oranges
200g/7oz/1 cup sugar
50ml/2fl oz/¼ cup cold water
100ml/3½fl oz/scant ½ cup

boiling water
100ml/3½fl oz/scant ½ cup fresh strong brewed coffee
50g/2oz/½ cup pistachio nuts, chopped (optional)

1 Finely pare the rind from one orange, shred and reserve the rind. Peel the remaining oranges. Cut each orange crossways into slices, then re-form and hold in place with a cocktail stick (toothpick) through the centre.

2 Put the sugar and cold water in a pan. Heat gently, stirring constantly, until the sugar dissolves, then bring to the boil and cook until the syrup turns a pale golden colour.

3 Remove from the heat and carefully pour the boiling water into the pan. Return to the heat until the syrup has dissolved in the water. Stir in the coffee.

4 Add the oranges and the shredded rind to the coffee syrup. Simmer for 15–20 minutes, turning the oranges once during cooking. Sprinkle with pistachio nuts, if using, and serve hot.

Cook's Tip
Choose a pan in which the oranges will just fit in a single layer.

Spiced Poached Kumquats

Kumquats are at their best just before the Christmas season. Simply poached with spices, their marvellous spicy-sweet citrus flavour produces a refreshing dish that will give any meal a lift.

Serves 6
450g/1lb/4 cups kumquats
115g/4oz/generous ½ cup caster (superfine) sugar
150ml/¼ pint/⅔ cup water
1 small cinnamon stick
1 star anise

1 Cut the kumquats in half and discard the seeds. Place the kumquats in a pan with the sugar, water and spices. Cook over a gentle heat, stirring until the sugar has dissolved.

2 Increase the heat, cover the pan and boil the mixture for 8–10 minutes until the kumquats are tender.

3 Transfer to a serving bowl, cool, then chill before serving.

Cook's Tip
To bottle the kumquats, spoon them into warm, sterilized jars at the end of step 2, then seal and label.

Crème Brûlée Energy 231Kcal/962kJ; Protein 5.7g; Carbohydrate 17.4g, of which sugars 17.4g; Fat 15.9g, of which saturates 8.5g; Cholesterol 190mg; Calcium 83mg; Fibre 0g; Sodium 50mg.
Oranges in Syrup Energy 183Kcal/782kJ; Protein 2g; Carbohydrate 46.4g, of which sugars 46.3g; Fat 0.1g, of which saturates 0g; Cholesterol 0mg; Calcium 84mg; Fibre 2.3g; Sodium 10mg.
Poached Kumquats Energy 103Kcal/441kJ; Protein 0.8g; Carbohydrate 26.6g, of which sugars 26.6g; Fat 0.1g, of which saturates 0g; Cholesterol 0mg; Calcium 33mg; Fibre 0.9g; Sodium 4mg.

Chocolate Fudge Bananas

A fast dessert that's bound to go down well with kids.

Serves 4
4 bananas
15ml/1 tbsp lemon juice
grated chocolate, to decorate

For the sauce
150ml/¼ pint/⅔ cup double (heavy) cream
50g/2oz/¼ cup butter
50g/2oz/¼ cup granulated sugar
175g/6oz plain (semisweet) chocolate, broken into pieces

1 Make the sauce. Heat the cream with the butter and sugar in the top of a double boiler or in a heatproof bowl over a pan of hot water. Stir until smooth, then remove from the heat and stir in the chocolate until combined.

2 Peel the bananas and cut into large pieces. Toss in the lemon juice, then arrange on individual plates and pour over the sauce. Top with grated chocolate and serve immediately.

Almost Instant Banana Pudding

Ginger cake is the base for this scrummy quick dessert.

Serves 6–8
4 thick slices ginger cake
6 bananas
30ml/2 tbsp lemon juice

300ml/½ pint/1¼ cups whipping cream or fromage frais
60ml/4 tbsp fruit juice
40–50g/1½–2oz/3–4 tbsp soft brown sugar

1 Break up the cake into chunks and arrange in an ovenproof dish. Peel and slice the bananas and toss in the lemon juice.

2 Whip the cream and, when firm, gently whip in the juice. (If using fromage frais, just gently stir in the juice.) Fold in the bananas and spoon the mixture over the ginger cake.

3 Top with the soft brown sugar and place under a hot grill (broiler) for 2–3 minutes to caramelize. Serve immediately.

Baked Bananas with Ice Cream

Baked bananas make the perfect partners for delicious vanilla ice cream topped with a toasted hazelnut sauce. A quick and easy dessert that looks as good as it tastes.

Serves 4
4 large bananas
15ml/1 tbsp lemon juice
4 large scoops vanilla ice cream

For the sauce
25g/1oz/2 tbsp unsalted (sweet) butter
50g/2oz/½ cup hazelnuts, toasted and roughly chopped
45ml/3 tbsp golden (light corn) syrup
30ml/2 tbsp lemon juice

1 Preheat the oven to 180°C/350°F/Gas 4. Place the unpeeled bananas on a baking sheet and brush them with the lemon juice. Bake for about 20 minutes until the skins are starting to turn black and the flesh gives a little when the bananas are gently squeezed.

2 Meanwhile, make the sauce. Melt the butter in a small pan. Add the hazelnuts and cook gently for 1 minute. Add the syrup and lemon juice and heat, stirring, for 1 minute more.

3 To serve, slit each banana open with a knife and open out the skins. Transfer to individual plates and serve with scoops of ice cream and the sauce poured over.

Cook's Tip
Cook the bananas over the dying coals of a barbecue, if you like. Put them on the rack as soon as you have removed all the main course items.

Variation
Use almonds instead of hazelnuts, and add a little brandy.

Chocolate Fudge Energy 647Kcal/2696kJ; Protein 4.1g; Carbohydrate 64.8g, of which sugars 62.1g; Fat 43g, of which saturates 26.5g; Cholesterol 81mg; Calcium 48mg; Fibre 2.2g; Sodium 89mg.
Banana Pudding Energy 326Kcal/1361kJ; Protein 3.1g; Carbohydrate 37.6g, of which sugars 30.4g; Fat 19.1g, of which saturates 11.6g; Cholesterol 39mg; Calcium 40mg; Fibre 1.1g; Sodium 106mg.
Baked Bananas Energy 416Kcal/1740kJ; Protein 6.3g; Carbohydrate 50.7g, of which sugars 47.2g; Fat 21.1g, of which saturates 9.5g; Cholesterol 35mg; Calcium 117mg; Fibre 1.9g; Sodium 124mg.

Barbecued Pineapple Boats with Rum Glaze

Fresh pineapple has even more flavour when barbecued; this spiced rum glaze turns it into a very special dessert in a matter of minutes.

Serves 4
1 medium pineapple, about 600g/1lb 6oz
25g/1oz/2 tbsp dark muscovado (molasses) sugar
5ml/1 tsp ground ginger
45ml/3 tbsp low-fat spread, melted
30ml/2 tbsp dark rum

1 With a large, sharp knife, cut the pineapple lengthways into four equal wedges.

2 Cut out and discard the hard centre core from each wedge of pineapple. Take care when handling the pineapple's rough outer skin.

3 Cut between the flesh and skin, to release the flesh; keep the skin in place. Slice the flesh across, into chunks.

4 Push a bamboo skewer lengthways through each wedge and into the stalk, to hold the chunks in place.

5 Mix together the sugar, ginger, melted spread and rum and then brush over the pineapple.

6 Cook the wedges on a hot barbecue for about 3–4 minutes.

7 Pour the remaining glaze over the top and serve.

Variation
For an even simpler version of this recipe, cut the skin off the pineapple and then slice the whole pineapple into thick slices and cook as above.

Deep-Fried Cherries

Succulent fresh cherries coated with a simple batter and then quickly deep-fried make a delicious and unusual dessert. Serve with vanilla ice cream for a perfect ending to a summery meal.

Serves 4–6
450g/1lb ripe red cherries, with stalks
225g/8oz packet batter mix
1 egg
vegetable oil, for deep-frying

1 Gently wash the cherries and pat dry with kitchen paper. Tie the stalks together with fine string to form clusters of four or five cherries.

2 Make up the batter mix according to the instructions on the packet, beating in the egg. Pour the vegetable oil into a deep-fat fryer or large, heavy pan and heat to 190°C/375°F.

3 Working in batches, half-dip each cherry cluster into the batter and then carefully drop the cluster into the hot oil. Fry for 3–4 minutes, or until golden.

4 Remove the deep-fried cherries with a wire-mesh skimmer or slotted spoon and drain on a wire rack placed over crumpled kitchen paper, and serve immediately.

Cook's Tips
• You can always make your own batter – it doesn't take much longer to put together. Sift 115g/4oz/1 cup plain (all-purpose) flour and a pinch of salt into a large bowl and make a well in the centre. Add 1 egg and 150ml/¼ pint/⅔ cup milk to the well and whisk them lightly together, then gradually whisk in the dry ingredients to make a smooth batter. You can flavour the batter with a little ground cinnamon, if you like.
• The cherry fritters taste even more delicious dusted with caster (superfine) sugar and served with whipped cream.

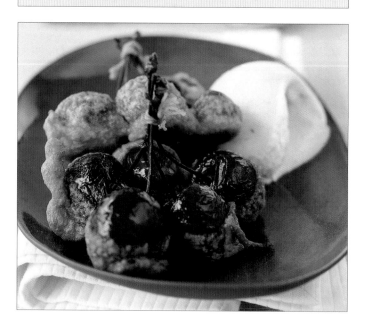

Pineapple & Rum Energy 455Kcal/1876kJ; Protein 1.4g; Carbohydrate 4.2g, of which sugars 4.2g; Fat 45.5g, of which saturates 28.3g; Cholesterol 116mg; Calcium 43mg; Fibre 0.4g; Sodium 55mg.
Deep-Fried Cherries Energy 250Kcal/1045kJ; Protein 4.5g; Carbohydrate 31.9g, of which sugars 9.1g; Fat 12.4g, of which saturates 1.6g; Cholesterol 32mg; Calcium 57mg; Fibre 1.6g; Sodium 13mg.

Grilled Nectarines with Amaretto

Amaretto, the sweet almond-flavoured liqueur from Italy, adds a touch of luxury to this incredibly quick and easy dessert.

Serves 4-6
6 ripe nectarines
30ml/2 tbsp clear honey
60ml/4 tbsp Amaretto di Saronno
half-fat crème fraîche, to serve
  (optional)

1 Cut the nectarines in half, running a small sharp knife down the side of each fruit from top to bottom, through to the stone (pit). Gently ease the halves apart and remove the stones.

2 Place the nectarines cut side up in a flameproof dish and drizzle 2.5ml/½ tsp honey and 5ml/1 tsp Amaretto over each half.

3 Preheat the grill (broiler) until very hot, then grill (broil) the fruit until slightly charred. Serve with crème fraîche, if you like.

Nectarines with Marzipan & Yogurt

A luscious dessert that few can resist; marzipan and nectarines are a wonderful combination. The nectarines can be cooked on the barbecue, if you like.

Serves 4
4 firm, ripe nectarines or peaches
75g/3oz marzipan
75ml/5 tbsp low-fat Greek
  (US strained plain) yogurt
3 amaretti, crushed

1 Cut the nectarines in half, running a small sharp knife down the side of each fruit through to the stone (pit). Gently ease the nectarine halves apart and remove the stones.

2 Cut the marzipan into eight pieces and press one piece into the cavity of each nectarine half. Preheat the grill (broiler).

3 Spoon the yogurt on top and sprinkle with crushed amaretti. Place the fruits under the hot grill. Cook for 3–5 minutes, until the yogurt starts to melt. Serve immediately.

Apples & Raspberries in Rose Syrup

Inspiration for this dessert stems from the fact that the apple and the raspberry belong to the rose family. The subtle flavours are shared here in an infusion of rose-scented tea.

Serves 4
5ml/1 tsp rose pouchong tea
900ml/1½ pints/3¾ cups
  boiling water
5ml/1 tsp rose water (optional)
50g/2oz/¼ cup granulated sugar
5ml/1 tsp lemon juice
5 eating apples
175g/6oz/1½ cups fresh
  raspberries

1 Warm a large tea pot. Add the rose pouchong tea, then pour on the boiling water, together with the rose water, if using. Allow to stand and infuse for 4 minutes.

2 Put the sugar and lemon juice into a stainless steel pan. Strain in the tea and stir to dissolve the sugar.

3 Peel and core the apples, then cut into quarters. Poach the apples in the syrup for about 5 minutes.

4 Transfer the apples and syrup to a large metal tray and leave to cool to room temperature.

5 Transfer the cooled apples and syrup to a bowl, add the raspberries and mix to combine. Spoon into individual dishes or bowls and serve warm.

Cook's Tip
Serve warm, not cold, to make the most of the delicate flavours.

Variation
Use orange blossom tea instead of the rose pouchong tea and replace the rose water with orange flower water.

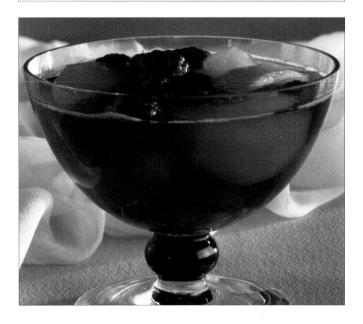

Grilled Nectarines Energy 93Kcal/394kJ; Protein 1.8g; Carbohydrate 18.8g, of which sugars 18.8g; Fat 0.1g, of which saturates 0g; Cholesterol 0mg; Calcium 10mg; Fibre 1.6g; Sodium 3mg. **Nectarines with Marzipan & Yogurt** Energy 161Kcal/682kJ; Protein 4.2g; Carbohydrate 28.5g, of which sugars 27.4g; Fat 4.4g, of which saturates 1.1g; Cholesterol 0mg; Calcium 49mg; Fibre 2.2g; Sodium 24mg. **Apples & Raspberries** Energy 104Kcal/447kJ; Protein 1.1g; Carbohydrate 26.2g, of which sugars 26.2g; Fat 0.3g, of which saturates 0.1g; Cholesterol 0mg; Calcium 23mg; Fibre 3.1g; Sodium 5mg.

Index

almond tart, 74
Amaretti: chocolate amaretti peaches, 14
Amaretto: grilled nectarines with Amaretto, 95
  roast peaches with Amaretto, 19
Apples: apple & walnut crumble, 32
  apple brown betty, 74
  apple charlottes, 28
  apple couscous pudding, 17
  apple foam with blackberries, 58
  apple fritters 23
  apple soufflé omelette, 27
  apple strudel, 33
  apples & raspberries in rose syrup, 95
  baked apples with apricot filling, 15
  baked apples with caramel sauce, 15
  baked apples with Marsala, 19
  chargrilled apples on cinnamon toasts, 89
  chunky apple bake, 72
  filo-topped apple pie, 30
  fresh fruit salad, 60
  frozen apple & blackberry terrine, 57
  plum, apple & banana scone pie, 74
  ruby fruit salad, 46
  spiced apple crumble, 33
  strawberry & apple crumble, 72
Apricots: apricot & orange jelly, 41
  apricot delight, 65
  apricot pancakes, 90
  apricot parcels, 31
  apricots in Marsala, 48
  apricots with orange cream, 38
  baked apples with apricot filling, 15
  banana & apricot caramel trifle, 40
  cinnamon & apricot soufflés, 65
  coconut dumplings with apricot sauce, 32
  quick apricot blender whip, 84
  three-fruit compote, 80
  yogurt with apricots & pistachios, 82
Autumn pudding, 51

Bananas: almost instant banana pudding, 93
  baked bananas with ice cream, 93
  banana & apricot caramel trifle, 40
  banana & mascarpone creams, 42
  banana & passion fruit whip, 84
  bananas with lime & cardamom sauce, 49
  barbecued bananas with spicy vanilla spread, 76
  Brazilian coffee bananas, 85
  Caribbean bananas, 77
  chocolate banana fool, 83
  chocolate chip banana pancakes, 14
  chocolate fudge bananas, 93
  fluffy banana & pineapple mousse, 59
  fried bananas, 25
  hot spiced bananas, 76
  plum, apple & banana scone pie, 74
  ruby fruit salad, 46
  toffee bananas, 25
  tropical fruit with maple butter, 26
Blackberries: apple foam with blackberries, 58
  blackberries in port, 80
  blackberry cobbler, 29
  frozen apple & blackberry terrine, 57
  lemon soufflé with blackberries, 37
  peach, blackberry & ice cream gratin, 81

Blackcurrants: blackcurrant & meringue trifles, 55
  blackcurrant sorbet, 35
  rich blackcurrant coulis, 58
  Russian fruit compote, 18
Blueberries: blueberry buckle, 75
  blueberry pancakes, 26
  hot blueberry & pear soufflés, 67
Brandy: mulled pears with ginger & brandy, 77
Bread: autumn pudding, 51
  bread & sultana custard, 68
  summer pudding, 51

Cherries: black cherry clafoutis, 29
  cherries jubilee, 21
  cherry pancakes, 78
  cherry syllabub, 41
  deep-fried cherries, 94
Chocolate: chocolate amaretti peaches, 14
  chocolate banana fool, 83
  chocolate chip banana pancakes, 14
  chocolate fudge bananas, 93
  chocolate mandarin trifle, 55
  peachy chocolate bake, 16
Christmas cranberry bombe, 56
Cider: warm pears in cider, 90
Clafoutis: black cherry, 29
Clementines: clementine jelly, 53
  fig, port & clementine sundaes, 40
  frozen clementines, 34
coconut dumplings with apricot sauce, 32
Coffee: Brazilian coffee bananas, 85
  coffee mascarpone creams, 83
  oranges in hot coffee syrup, 92
compote: baked fruit compote, 73
  three-fruit compote, 80
Cornflake-topped peach bake, 75
Couscous: apple couscous pudding, 17
Cranberries: Christmas cranberry bombe, 56
Crème brûlée, 92
Custard: bread & sultana custard, 68
  grilled pineapple with rum custard, 91
  poppyseed custard with red fruit, 68

date & tofu ice, 60

Elderflower: elderflower & lime yogurt ice, 36
  gooseberry & elderflower fool, 53
Figs: fig, port & clementine sundaes, 40
  figs with ricotta cream, 85
  fresh fig filo tart, 30
  fresh figs with honey and wine, 73
  Greek fig & honey pudding, 89
  warm autumn compote, 21
Filo pastry: apple strudel, 33
  apricot parcels, 31
  crispy mango stacks with raspberry coulis, 64
  filo-topped apple pie, 30
  filo chiffon pie, 66
  fresh fig filo tart, 30
Fools: chocolate banana fool, 83
  gooseberry & elderflower fool, 53
  mango & lime fool, 52
  rhubarb and orange 38,
fritters: apple 23
frudités with honey dip, 84
fruit preparation, 10–11

Ginger: ginger & orange crème brûlée, 92
  mango & ginger clouds, 67
  mulled pears with ginger & brandy, 77
  papaya baked with ginger, 20
  peach & ginger pashka, 54
  rhubarb & ginger trifles, 88
  watermelon, ginger & grapefruit salad, 87
Gooseberries: crunchy gooseberry crumble, 79
  gooseberry & elderflower fool, 53
  gooseberry & orange flower cream, 39
Grapefruit: grapefruit in honey & whisky, 87
  watermelon, ginger & grapefruit salad, 87

Grapes: grapes in grape-yogurt jelly, 62
  ruby fruit salad, 46
  strawberries in spiced grape jelly, 61

Honey: fresh figs with honey & wine, 73
  frudités with honey dip, 84
  grapefruit in honey & whisky, 87
  Greek fig & honey pudding, 89

Ice cream: baked bananas with ice cream, 93
  peach, blackberry & ice cream gratin, 81
  pineapple crush ice cream, 81
  summer fruit salad ice cream, 56

kiwis: exotic fruit salad with passion fruit dressing, 46
  fragrant fruit salad, 43
  fruit kebabs with mango & yogurt sauce, 44
Kumquats: kumquat compote, 73
  spiced poached kumquats, 92

Lemons: lemon coeur à la crème with Cointreau oranges, 42
  lemon hearts with strawberry sauce, 71
  lemon posset, 83
  lemon soufflé with blackberries, 37
  lemon surprise pudding, 17
Limes: bananas with lime & cardamom sauce, 49
  elderflower & lime yogurt ice, 36
  mango & lime fool, 52

Mandarins: chocolate mandarin trifle, 55
  mandarins in orange flower syrup, 63
Mango: crispy mango stacks with raspberry coulis, 64
  exotic fruit salad with passion fruit dressing, 46
  fragrant fruit salad, 43
  fruit kebabs with mango & yogurt sauce, 44
  mango & ginger clouds, 67
  mango & lime fool, 52
  mangoes with sticky rice, 47
  tropical fruit gratin, 20
  tropical fruit with maple butter, 26
Maple syrup: tropical fruit with maple butter, 26
Marsala: apricots in Marsala, 48
  baked apples with Marsala, 19
Marzipan: nectarines with marzipan & yogurt, 95
Mascarpone: apricots with orange cream, 38
  banana & mascarpone creams, 42
  coffee mascarpone creams, 83
  stuffed peaches with mascarpone cream, 22
melon: ruby fruit salad, 46
  three-fruit compote, 80

Nectarines: grilled nectarines with Amaretto, 95
  grilled nectarines with ricotta & spice, 78
  nectarines with marzipan & yogurt, 95

Orange flower water: gooseberry & orange flower cream, 39
  mandarins in orange flower syrup, 63
  orange-blossom jelly, 62
Oranges: apricot & orange jelly, 41
  apricots with orange cream, 38
  chilled oranges in syrup, 63
  fresh citrus jelly, 61
  fresh fruit salad, 60
  ginger & orange crème brûlée, 92
  lemon coeur à la crème with Cointreau oranges, 42
  orange & yogurt ice, 34
  orange yogurt brûlées, 69
  oranges in hot coffee syrup, 92
  oranges with caramel wigs, 49
  pistachio & rose water oranges, 88
  prune & orange pots, 86
  rhubarb & orange fool, 38
  scented red & orange fruit salad, 88
  souffléed orange semolina, 66

Papayas: exotic fruit salad with passion fruit dressing, 46
  fragrant fruit salad, 43
  golden pineapple with papaya sauce, 24
  papaya baked with ginger, 20
  papayas in jasmine flower syrup, 45
  tropical fruit with maple butter, 26
Passion fruit: banana & passion fruit whip, 84
  exotic fruit salad with passion fruit dressing, 46
  fragrant fruit salad, 43
  passion fruit soufflés, 89
  raspberry passion fruit swirls, 70
Pastry making, 8–9
Peaches: baked lattice peaches, 22
  chocolate amaretti peaches, 14
  cornflake-topped peach bake, 75
  fresh fruit salad, 60
  peach & ginger pashka, 54
  peach, blackberry & ice cream gratin, 81
  peach cobbler, 16
  peach melba syllabub, 43
  peachy chocolate bake, 16
  roast peaches with Amaretto, 19
  stuffed peaches with mascarpone cream, 22
Pears: hot blueberry & pear soufflés, 67
  mulled pears with ginger & brandy, 77
  poached pears in port syrup, 45
  warm autumn compote, 21
  warm pears in cider, 90
Pies: filo chiffon pie, 66
  one-crust rhubarb pie, 31
  plum, apple & banana scone pie, 74
Pineapples: barbecued pineapple boats with rum glaze, 94
  fluffy banana & pineapple mousse, 59
  fragrant fruit salad, 43
  fresh pineapple salad, 86
  fruit kebabs with mango & yogurt sauce, 44
  golden pineapple with papaya sauce, 24
  grilled pineapple with rum custard, 91
  pineapple crush ice cream, 81
  pineapple flambé, 91
  Thai fried pineapple, 24
  three-fruit compote, 80
  tropical fruit gratin, 20
Pistachios: pistachio & rose water oranges, 88
  yogurt with apricots & pistachios, 82
Plums: floating islands in a hot plum sauce, 77
  plum & port sorbet, 57
  plum, apple & banana scone pie, 74
  ruby plum mousse, 52
Pomegranates: fragrant fruit salad, 43
  minted pomegranate yogurt, 80
Poppyseed custard with red fruit, 68
Port: blackberries in port, 80
  fig, port & clementine sundaes, 40
  plum & port sorbet, 57
  poached pears in port syrup, 45
  ruby plum mousse, 52
Prunes: prune & orange pots, 86
  prunes poached in red wine, 48
Puddings: almost instant banana pudding, 93
  apple couscous pudding, 17
  autumn pudding, 51
  Greek fig & honey pudding, 89
  lemon surprise pudding, 17
  rice pudding with mixed berry sauce, 71
  summer pudding, 51

Raspberries: apples & raspberries in rose syrup, 95
  crispy mango stacks with raspberry coulis, 64
  frozen French raspberry mousse, 54
  minted raspberry bavarois, 59
  raspberry passion fruit swirls, 70
  raspberry trifle, 37
  raspberry yogurt layer, 82
  red fruit coulis with meringue, 85
  toffee berry brûlée, 69

tofu berry "cheesecake", 79
  warm autumn compote, 21
Redcurrants: red fruit coulis with meringue, 85
Russian fruit compote, 44
Rhubarb: filo chiffon pie, 66
  one-crust rhubarb pie, 31
  rhubarb & ginger trifles, 88
  rhubarb & orange fool, 38
  rhubarb spiral cobbler, 28
  rhubarb-strawberry crisp, 27
Rice: mangoes with sticky rice, 47
  rice pudding with mixed berry sauce, 71
Ricotta: figs with ricotta cream, 85
  fruity ricotta creams, 39
  grilled nectarines with ricotta & spice, 78
Rose petals: strawberry rose petal pashka, 70
Rum: barbecued pineapple boats with rum glaze, 94
  grilled pineapple with rum custard, 91
  hot bananas with rum & raisins, 23

Sauces, 12–13
Semolina: souffléed orange, 66
Star anise fruits with coconut jelly, 50
Strawberries: fresh fruit salad, 60
  fruit-filled soufflé omelette, 90
  fruit kebabs with mango & yogurt sauce, 44
  lemon hearts with strawberry sauce, 71
  poppyseed custard with red fruit, 68
  rhubarb-strawberry crisp, 27
  scented red & orange fruit salad, 88
  summer berry frozen yogurt, 36
  summer fruit salad ice cream, 56
  strawberries in spiced grape jelly, 61
  strawberries with Cointreau, 64
  strawberry & apple crumble, 76
  strawberry rose petal pashka, 70
  tofu berry "cheesecake", 79
Summer pudding, 51

Tangerine trifle, 37
Tarts: almond tart, 74
  fresh fig filo tart, 30
Toffee bananas, 25
Tofu: date & tofu ice, 60
  toffee berry brûlée, 69
  tofu berry "cheesecake" 79

Walnuts: apple & walnut crumble, 32
Watermelon: watermelon, ginger & grapefruit salad, 87
  watermelon ice, 36
  watermelon sorbet, 35
Wine: fresh figs with honey & wine, 73
  prunes poached in red wine, 48

Yogurt: elderflower & lime yogurt ice, 36
  fruit kebabs with mango & yogurt sauce, 44
  grapes in grape-yogurt jelly, 62
  minted pomegranate yogurt, 80
  nectarines with marzipan & yogurt, 95
  orange & yogurt ice, 34
  orange yogurt brûlées, 69
  raspberry yogurt layer, 82
  summer berry frozen yogurt, 36
  yogurt with apricots & pistachios, 82